The
Marshall Cavendish

International
WILDLIFE
ENCYCLOPEDIA

VOLUME 4
BLA –BUZ

MARSHALL CAVENDISH
NEW YORK · LONDON · TORONTO · SYDNEY

Revised Edition Published 1991

Published by Marshall Cavendish Corporation
2415 Jerusalem Avenue
North Bellmore, NY 11710
USA

Printed and bound in Italy by LEGO Spa Vicenza

Library of Congress Cataloging-in-Publication Data

Marshall Cavendish International wildlife encyclopedia/general
 editors, Maurice Burton and Robert Burton.
  p. cm.
  "Portions of this work have also been published as The
International wildlife encyclopedia, Encyclopedia of animal life and
Funk & Wagnalls wildlife encyclopedia."
  Includes index.
  Contents: v. 4. BLA-BUZ.
  ISBN 0-86307-734-X (set).
  ISBN 0-86307-738-2 (v. 4).
  1. Zoology–Collected works. I. Burton, Maurice, 1898-
II. Burton, Robert, 1941-   . III. Title: International wildlife
encyclopedia.
QL3.M35 1988
591′.03′21–dc 19

Volume 4

Black bear

There are five species of black bear, each placed in a separate genus. All are smaller than the brown bears, and all are sufficiently similar for one of them, the one most studied, to serve as a type for the other four. This is the American black bear which originally inhabited practically all the wooded areas of North America from Central Mexico northwards. Its numbers are much reduced now and it has been eliminated from much of its former range, but in national parks its numbers are increasing and elsewhere it survives close to human settlement. Up to 5 ft long with a 4½ in. tail, and weighing 200 – 500 lb, it has shorter fur, shorter claws and shorter hind feet than the brown bears. The species also shows a number of colour phases: black, chocolate brown, cinnamon brown, blue-black and white with buff on the head and in the middle of the back. This last is most common in British Columbia, where it has been known as Kermode's bear. These different colour phases may occur in the same litter.

Friendly habits

Black bears are good tree climbers, powerful, quick to react, harmless to people except when provoked, cornered or injured – or through sheer friendliness. In national parks, where they are familiar with human beings and come begging food, visitors to the parks must keep to the protection of cars to avoid inadvertent injury from the bears' claws. Black bears are solitary except during the breeding season, the two partners separating after mating, to wander far in search of food. The American black bear sleeps through the winter – not hibernation in the usual sense – after laying in fat by heavy autumn feeding. It does not feed during the winter although it may leave its den, a hollow tree or similar shelter, for brief excursions during mild spells. When startled, the adult gives a 'woof', otherwise it is silent. The cubs, when distressed, utter shrill howls.

Mixed diet

Insects, berries and fruits, eggs and young of ground-nesting birds, rodents and carrion form its main foods, but young of deer and pronghorn are killed and eaten. Porcupines are killed, the bear flipping them over with its paw and attacking the soft under-belly, often to its own detriment from the quills. Black bears have been found dead with quills embedded in the mouth. Sometimes a black bear may turn cattle-killer.

Enemies

Old or sickly adults are occasionally killed by pumas and wintering bears may be attacked by wolves.

Michigan Dept Conservation

△ *Black bear advancing rather quickly towards the photographer. On the whole they are friendly animals, only becoming aggressive when provoked, cornered or injured. In the national parks of America they beg for food.*

Life history

The breeding month is June and the gestation period is 100 to 210 days. Usually there are two or three cubs in a litter, exceptionally four, rarely five, born in January and February. At birth the 8 in., 9 – 12 oz cubs are blind, toothless and naked except for scanty

American black bear *(Euarctos americanus)*

dark hair. The mother continues to sleep for two months after the birth, having roused herself sufficiently to bite through the umbilical cords. The cubs alternately suck and sleep during these two months. They stay with the mother for at least six months, and she mates only every other year.

The original Teddy Bear

In 1902, Theodore (Teddy) Roosevelt, who was a keen naturalist as well as President of the United States, captured a black bear cub on a hunting trip, which he adopted as a pet. Morris Michton, a Brooklyn doll manufacturer, used this bear as model for the first Teddy Bear, so named with the President's permission. The popularity of the Teddy Bear as a toy was immediate and world-wide. The black bear, as already stated, is such a favourite in American national parks that they take liberties with visitors. In European zoos a prime favourite with visitors is the Himalayan black bear. Such general favouritism owes much to the human-like qualities of the bears.

We tend to favour in animals, qualities which reflect our own, as with birds that talk or animals that stand erect such as penguins, owls and bears. In man the bipedal stance is habitual; in bears it is but occasional, the usual way of walking being on all-fours. That does not invalidate the comparison, and the effect of the bears' ability to stand erect at times is reinforced by the way they will sit upright, as if on a chair, and also by the characteristic way a bear will wave a fore-paw (or hand) when soliciting food. Another trait which enables us to see ourselves in bears is their way of lying prone, on their backs.

Bears also appear to be intelligent. Whether they are more intelligent than their near relatives, the cats and dogs, has never been adequately tested. At least we know that the cubs stay with the mother for six months, often longer, and some may stay with her until her next cubs are born. A long period of parental care allows for learning by example and a longer period for experience with security. And if bears are by nature solitary they can, if circumstances compel them, as in bear-pits in zoos, live together with little discord, showing they are, like us, fundamentally friendly.

Yet in spite of the comparisons that can be drawn between bears and ourselves, and in spite of our fondness for Teddy Bears, the fact remains that the American black bear, like all other bears, has long been a target for the hunter's gun.

class	**Mammalia**
order	**Carnivora**
family	**Ursidae**
genus & species	*Euarctos americanus* American black bear

Okapia

If you go down to the woods today . . .

△ *Black bear surveying the scene from the undergrowth. This upright stance is used but on occasion, the usual way of walking being on all fours. In zoos most bears have learnt to use this ability of being able to stand erect with advantage. They beg and even wave their forepaws to attract a crowd and then get lots of food thrown to them.*

▷ *Black bear going for a brief excursion from its winter den. They do not hibernate in the usual sense, but sleep for long periods, leaving the den during mild spells. They do not eat but rely on fat stored by heavy autumn feeding.*

▽ *Twin cubs being escorted by their mother. They stay with her until at least 6 months old.*

Joe Van Worner: Photo Res.

Joe Van Worner: Photo Res.

Blackbird

A member of the thrush family ranging over Europe and its adjacent islands, with races in Asia and in North Africa, the Azores, Madeira and the Canaries. The male is 10 in. long, with a glossy black plumage and an orange bill. The female differs in being umber-brown on the back, reddish-brown on the underparts with dark spots and a whitish throat. Her beak is dark brown but may have some yellow on it. The first year juveniles are like the hen but lighter, more reddish and the mottling of the underparts is more pronounced. Partial albinism is common, most pronounced in males, from white patches on the wings or on the throat, to give, in extreme cases, a piebald plumage.

The American blackbirds include several species of insect-eating members of the family Icteridae, which includes orioles and grackles. In these the plumage is predominantly black but otherwise they have no affinity with the European blackbird.

Nature's sentinel

A rattle-like alarm note which readily alerts other birds to a predator or an intruder is a characteristic feature of the blackbird. This is a bird of hedgerows, shrubberies and thickets, and is common on farms and in gardens. Although often present in large numbers in a small area, it is not gregarious but will roost in considerable numbers at times in plantations, thickets or well-grown hedgerows. In fact the blackbird is one of the few wild birds presently increasing in numbers, as shown by the British Trust for Ornithology's Nest Record Survey. It is doing particularly well in suburban gardens, probably because food on bird tables is cutting down the normal winter toll of deaths. On the ground a blackbird runs or hops, stopping every few yards. The males especially are aggressive towards each other at all times of the year. In spring this is more pronounced and may be the cause of blackbirds seen running or flying in line, half-a-dozen at a time.

The song, which begins in late February or March, sometimes as early as December, continues until early July. It is a rich fluty song, usually delivered from well up in a tree. Blackbirds generally live in one place but there is some short distance migration, especially among juveniles.

Food

Berries and soft fruits are especially taken and the blackbird can be very destructive among strawberries and gooseberry and currant bushes. Seeds and grain are also eaten, as well as insects and their grubs, earthworms, spiders, millipedes and small snails. A blackbird searches for its animal food by turning over leaf litter, mainly with the bill, sometimes with the feet.

Hawks and owls, as well as small ground predators, especially domestic cats, will attack the blackbird. A high proportion of birds killed on roads by motor traffic are blackbirds.

Life history

The nest is usually built a few feet up from the ground in bushes, but may be on the ground or high up in trees. More often built by the hen alone, it is cup-shaped, of grass, leaves and roots, often with moss, cemented and lined with mud but with an inner lining of dry grass. The eggs, 3–5, rarely up to 9, are bluish-green freckled with reddish-brown or boldly marked with red-brown and grey. Breeding begins early, in March, often before wintry weather is past, but becomes more general in April. Normally it ends in July, after two or three broods, but exceptionally there may be five broods, the last in late summer. Incubation, by the hen alone, lasts two weeks. The young as nestlings and as fledglings out of the nest, are fed by both parents for a total of 2 weeks, mainly with earthworms.

The hen blackbird is sometimes mistaken for a thrush, because of its speckled breast.

Norman Duerden

Blackbird mysteries

Although blackbirds are so common, and are familiar in parks and gardens even in large towns, much of their behaviour remains unstudied. There is, however, one aspect more especially that remains unresolved: whether blackbirds and thrushes ever hybridise. Under natural conditions there is little hybridisation in any land animals, although ducks are known to do so, especially where two or more species have their breeding grounds on large lakes. Reports of blackbird-thrush crosses are not infrequent and these are almost impossible to prove or disprove. It is, however, almost certain that they arise from the variation in the speckling or mottling of the hen. Not infrequently someone, perhaps an interested layman, reports seeing a cock blackbird, unmistakable from his black plumage and yellow bill, courting a thrush and eventually mating with her. Other reports tell of a cock blackbird and a hen song thrush feeding a brood of fledglings that seem to be half-blackbird and half-thrush. It is significant that no reports tell of a cock thrush behaving in this way towards a hen blackbird.

The solution seems to lie in the observer being unfamiliar with the extent to which colour in animals, and colour patterns, normally vary. If one visits a museum whose cabinets contain large collections of bird skins and lays a score or so skins of hen blackbirds and a similar number of thrush skins on the table belly uppermost, the cause of the deception becomes obvious. The dark spots on a hen blackbird are usually small and most obvious on the throat only. Those of the hen thrush are large, well-spaced and distributed over the whole of the underside. But in some hen blackbirds the spots are larger and more conspicuous than usual and are continued down over the belly. Such birds look very thrush-like. With a series of skins laid out on a table, one is in no doubt which are blackbird and which are thrush. Nevertheless, it is easy to believe that, when viewing these birds from a distance, mistaken identity could come easily.

So also with the fledglings. Where there is greater variation in the spots than usual,

Cock blackbird tidying the nest by removing a faecal pellet from it.

Jane Burton: Photo Res.

in a brood of four or five, one or more of the young blackbirds may look very thrush-like yet have the darker colouring of a blackbird. Faced with such a brood even the experienced ornithologist cannot always be positive that he is not looking at a group of hybrids.

The situation is not helped by the eggs. The colour of blackbirds' and thrushes' eggs are not markedly different and those of blackbirds, particularly, are prone to vary in pattern as well as colour, so a nest may seem to have half blackbird eggs and half thrush eggs. But this can happen when both parents are known to be blackbirds.

Perhaps the most decisive evidence is in the nest. It is the hen in both species that build the nest. So if there were cross-mating between a hen thrush and a cock blackbird, the nest would be built on the thrush pattern and would be unmistakable. The song thrush's nest, similar to a blackbird's, can be distinguished by its lining of dung or rotten wood mixed with saliva.

class	**Aves**
order	**Passeriformes**
family	**Turdidae**
genus & species	***Turdus merula*** *(European blackbird)*

Blackbuck

Also known as the Indian antelope, it is just under 4 ft long, 2½ ft at the shoulder and weighs up to 80 lb. It is one of the few antelopes in which the male differs from the female in coloration. The buck is a rich dark brown on the upper parts and the outsides of the legs, with white underparts and white round the eyes. In the doe the dark brown is replaced by yellowish-fawn. Only the buck has horns and these are ringed and spirally twisted, up to 2 ft 4 in. long. The narrow sheep-like muzzle is white. The tail is short and the hooves delicate and sharply pointed. The range of the blackbuck includes West Pakistan and India from Kathiawar to Bengal, including the Punjab, and south-ward to Cape Cormorin.

Fastest jumper on the Indian plains

Blackbuck are extremely swift, one of the fastest of land animals, credited with speeds of 50 mph and able to outrun the fastest greyhound. They can take strides of 19—22 ft between hoofprints. When suddenly alarmed, first one quickly followed by others will leap over 6 ft into the air, like the impala and springbok in Africa. This bounding is continued for a while after which the herd settles down to a gallop. The antelope lives usually on flat open plains. Blackbuck are

A small feeding herd of female blackbuck.

seen in herds of up to 50 although herds of several hundreds have been recorded. Each of the small herds is attended by a single buck, but it is the does that alert the herd to danger.

Feeding

Blackbuck rest in shade during the heat of the day, but otherwise spend their time cropping grass or troubling farmers by eating cereal crops where available.

Male blackbucks resting. The one on the left is a mature buck seen from his dark brown coat and long spirally twisted horns. The younger male will become like this as he matures.

Life history

Each adult buck serves a harem of does from which rival males are driven away. Mating is in February and March, and gestation lasts 180 days, producing a single young or sometimes twins. As the young males reach maturity, the old buck drives them from the herd and they live for a while in bachelor groups before each acquires its own harem. The life-span is up to 15 years.

Eclipse of the blackbuck

The blackbuck forms one of the signs of the Indian zodiac, and unless reasonable conservation measures are continued it may become as legendary as some of the signs of other zodiacs. The antelope must once have existed in vast numbers. Even fifty years ago Lyddeker was writing of herds of hundreds or even thousands. Today, the talk is of small herds living in reserves and of blackbuck being scarce outside these.

The traditional sport of princes and nobles has been hunting the blackbuck with cheetah. The Mogul Emperor Akbar, in the 16th century, is said to have kept 1 000 cheetahs for hunting. The cheetah was taken hooded in an ox-cart, to where black-buck were grazing. The hood was removed and the cheetah freed. If the cheetah failed to catch up with a blackbuck in the first 100 yd or so it gave up and sat on its haunches, but should it make a kill it was given a drink of the antelope's blood.

With the British occupation of India, shooting blackbuck became a favourite sport. Major FG Alexander, writing in 1911, told of shooting over 200 blackbuck as part of his hunting exploits, and there must have been many other British officers who could have told of similar experiences. At the same time he indicated that poaching was rife, the local people using snares made of strips of antelope hide or holding drives in which beaters guided the antelopes to-

wards hidden marksmen with muzzle-loaders. This, probably more than any other form of persecution, has led to the eclipse of the blackbuck. The late EP Gee, whose knowledge of the Indian fauna was probably unrivalled, drew attention a few years ago to the widespread poaching still continuing and to the consequent scarcity of blackbuck throughout its range. Indeed, he suggested that the loss of the blackbuck and a few other game animals had led to the virtual extinction of the Indian cheetah too.

There is some doubt about the identity of the animal on which the legend of the uni-corn was based. Some name the rhinoceros, others the oryx but there are those who suggest that it is the blackbuck. It is not un-common for one horn on a buck to be de-formed and curled like a ram's horn, or to be completely atrophied, giving a one-horned hoofed animal with the ringed horn similar to that of the legendary unicorn of heraldry. No one has ever seen a real live unicorn. Future generations may never have the chance to see a live blackbuck.

class	**Mammalia**
order	**Artiodactyla**
family	**Bovidae**
genus & species	***Antilope cervicapra***

Blackbuck *(Antilope cervicapra)*

Black-headed gull

This is a very familiar bird, common not only around shores, but also inland where it may be seen following ploughs or searching for scraps in towns. The black-headed gull is one of the smaller gulls and is distinguished from other gulls, in Britain and most of Europe at least, by the chocolate-brown 'hood' on its head. There are other gulls with similar hoods, such as the Mediterranean gull and the laughing gull of the east coast of the United States.

The body is white with grey back and wings. The wing tips are black and the bill and legs red. Only mature black-headed gulls have the hood, the young birds having only a mottled brown cap on the crown. In winter the hood disappears except for small patches on the sides of the head and in front of the eyes.

Black-headed gulls are found over most of Europe and Asia. In Europe they are absent from the north of Scandinavia and Russia and are found in the Mediterranean countries only during the winter. Some black-headed gulls migrate, moving south in winter, and occasionally they make longer journeys. Individuals have been recorded from Greenland, along the east coast of America, to Mexico.

Scavenging opens a new way of life

Although often called 'sea-gulls', gulls normally live around coasts, rarely being found out to sea, and many are now found inland. The black-headed gull is especially common inland, and inland breeding colonies have recently become established in several places in Britain.

This is because black-headed gulls are scavengers missing no chance to get food, and town waste tips often close to arable land are providing new opportunities for the birds to feed inland. They sometimes hunt for flying insects and will catch night-flying moths as they come out in the evening. Along the shores they search for food in shallow water by plunge-diving, dropping on the water to immerse head and breast but never becoming completely submerged. They will also paddle, marking time with their feet, on wet sand or mud to make worms come to the surface. Shore animals such as sand-eels, shrimps and winkles, form an important part of the diet, as do worms and insects on land.

Black-headed gulls will occasionally eat small birds and mice and will also rob nests of eggs and nestlings, including those of their own kind. Coots and ducks are robbed of food as they surface from a dive and lapwings have their food snatched before they can swallow it.

The diet also includes plants such as grass, moss and seaweed, cereal crops, potatoes and turnips.

Thousands breed together

Several thousand pairs of the black-headed gulls may nest close together in one colony. Most nests are only 2–3 ft apart, giving the gulls just enough room to live without coming into conflict with their neighbours. Such colonial nesting is common among gulls.

In early March, flocks of black-headed gulls congregate near the colonies and pay short visits to them during the day. These visits become longer and longer until the eggs are laid. Even then the eggs are left overnight. The reason for this unwillingness to stay in the colony, which is sometimes shown by the whole flock suddenly taking to the air and flying away, is that sitting packed together in the colony, the gulls are an easy prey for predators such as foxes. A single fox can wreak havoc in a gull colony overnight, so the gulls avoid staying in the colony until the need to incubate continuously makes it essential. Towards the end of the breeding season, the adults again take to leaving the colony overnight, so abandoning the fledglings to any predator.

The nest is made of grass or other vegetation. Often it is just a depression scraped in the ground and roughly lined. Three brown eggs, with black spots and blotches, are laid. Sometimes four and very rarely six are laid, but no more than three are likely to hatch because the gulls have only three brood patches. These are patches of bare skin on the breast, richly supplied with blood vessels, against which the eggs are

Black-headed gull taking off from its roosting grounds where it may also feed. This gull's scavenging way of life has brought it inland in recent years to feed on rubbish tips and farmland but it still feeds by plunge-diving for fish, its calls attracting other gulls from far and wide (see overleaf).

Arthur Christiansen

Roy A Harris & KR Duff

△ *Black-headed gulls in winter plunge-diving into water to catch small fish.*
▷ *Black-headed gull at its untidy nest. The black head is characteristic of its summer plumage only, when gulls are breeding, and is related to courtship displays.*
▽ *Gull over farmland searching for food. In winter it does not have a black head.*

Roy A Harris & KR Duff

André Fatras

E Herbert: AFA

Black-headed gull attending to the nest. A chick on the left has just penetrated its shell.

Eric Hosking

Parent with regurgitated food in its beak for the chick. At 5 weeks the chick learns to fly.

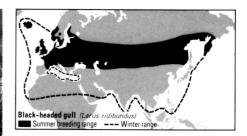

Black-headed gull *(Larus ridibundus)*
■ Summer breeding range --- Winter range

Gulls on the move

As well as the migration between summer and winter ranges, see map, these gulls commute daily between feeding and roosting grounds. From raucous daytime flocks behind ploughs and over fields, they form long straggling Vs of gulls idling their way home high in the evening sky.

placed to keep them warm. Both parents incubate the eggs, taking spells of several hours each.

The chicks hatch out 3 weeks after the eggs are laid and are able to walk around after a few hours, but at first they do not go far from the nest. The parents bring food back to the nest and regurgitate it on to the ground for the chicks to peck at for themselves. The chicks learn to fly at 5 weeks and leave the colony to join the adults at the feeding grounds and roosts.

Enemies dive-bombed

Black-headed gulls were once regarded as a delicacy. Young birds were even taken from the colonies and fattened in special gullhouses. The taste for black-headed gulls has died out, however, but until recent protection laws eggs were collected by the thousand and sold as plovers' eggs.

Black-headed gulls suffer from two types of enemy. One attacks from the air, the other on the ground. The reaction to the former, which includes hawks and other birds of prey, is for the gulls to rise in a dense flock and fly about with frequent changes of direction. This hinders the predator's efforts to single out any single gull to attack.

Birds of prey do not usually molest the eggs or chicks of gulls, but crows and the larger species of gull such as herring and black-backed gulls will search for unattended eggs and nestlings. Mammals also invade the colonies and their forays can be traced by the remains of adult gulls, nestlings and empty egg shells. Foxes are particularly dangerous to gulls, especially on very dark nights when the birds cannot see them. A fox will kill many more gulls than it can eat, leaving some corpses unmutilated and burying others. Although of no danger to adult gulls hedgehogs will forage through the colony breaking eggs and sucking their contents. They also kill and eat young chicks. Unfortunately the chicks' reaction to danger is to freeze. This may cause some predators to overlook them but it is a poor form of defence against a hedgehog, which hunts by smell.

The reactions of the adult gulls to these enemies depends on how much danger they present to the gulls themselves. Hedgehogs

and crows which do not attack adult gulls are subjected to 'dive-bombing' attacks by the gulls which sometimes strike them with their feet. Foxes, on the other hand, are treated with more respect. The gulls hover over them uttering alarm calls and only occasionally swooping past in 'dive-bomb' attacks, which are not pressed home.

Bird commuters

Over the centuries, London has attracted an ever-increasing population of humans, large numbers of whom do not live in London itself but commute each day from the suburbs. Some of these commuters may have noticed that there is another animal commuting with them. This is the black-headed gull. Every morning and evening, straggling flocks of them can be seen flying leisurely over the suburbs of London. In the morning they fly into the centre to feed. Parks, where people hand out offerings of bread to any birds willing to eat it, the River Thames, rubbish dumps, railway sidings and playing fields all provide the gulls with food, and like the house sparrows and pigeons, the gulls have become efficient exploiters of man.

In the evening the gulls move out of London, returning to their roosts on sewage farms, lakes and reservoirs around the outskirts. Of the tens of thousands of gulls that forage in various parts of London during the day, half go out westwards to the Staines-Windsor area and the others go out eastwards to the Lea Valley. The return trip is as regular as any performed by people working in the City. By ringing the gulls it has been shown that each bird goes to the same feeding place every day and returns to the same roost at night.

The daily journey takes place in only the winter months, for in spring the gulls of London return to their breeding colonies along the coasts. It is only within the last century that they have been coming inland. Previously black-headed gulls were rarely seen along the Thames above London Docks, but after some hard winters from 1887–1895 black-headed gulls started coming up the Thames. It is said that the first movement upriver was the result of gulls finding fish offal around Billingsgate Market in the City

of London. This, so we are told, caught the attention of Londoners, who started feeding the birds from London Bridge. The gulls responded readily, and the habit of feeding them was reported from bridge after bridge until finally the gulls had reached Putney or beyond. From the river they started to spread through London, gradually losing contact with the water. Some have come to stay. There is, for example, a small breeding colony on a sewage farm hard by London Airport.

The precise details of how the gulls have changed their behaviour and found their way up the Thames have never been documented, but it is easy to visualise how their own pattern of feeding could have helped. In the Thames today, between Richmond Bridge and Teddington, for example, a shoal of small fish may suddenly appear at the surface. At that moment the black-headed gulls will be spread out thinly, each bird busy with its own particular activities. One gull sees the small fishes breaking surface and dives down to feed on them, calling as it does so. Immediately the few other gulls in the immediate vicinity fly in to join in the feast, also calling. In no time at all, gulls can be seen streaming from Richmond to the east and from Teddington to the west so that an excited flock, wheeling and diving, assembles over the shoal and moves downstream with the fishes. Suddenly the small fishes go deeper, the flock of gulls breaks up, and its individual members fly back to where they were before the excitement started, having made a journey of anything up to a mile in order to take part in the feeding assembly.

We have only to replace the shoal of fishes with a few people throwing food for the gulls from one of London's bridges to see how a similar response by the gulls could have taken them farther upstream.

class	**Aves**
order	**Charadriiformes**
family	**Laridae**
genus & species	*Larus ridibundus* *black-headed gull*

Black molly

This is a black variety of a live-bearing tooth-carp of the family Cyprinodontidae. It occurs naturally in three out of the eight species of Mollienisia. It has been selectively bred by fish fanciers, and both the black variety and the naturally-coloured forms are favoured by aquarists. It is chosen here to represent the peculiarities of several species of Mollienisia. All 'mollies' are small, 2—5 in. long, live in Central American rivers, and are characterised by having a large rounded tail and a prominent dorsal fin. This, in the male, is extra large and sail-like. The biology of all species of Mollienisia is similar.

Aggressive fin display

The most interesting feature of black mollies is their large dorsal fin like a sail, which is used in aggressive displays and in courtship. Rival males swim at each other with all fins expanded, but the fin display is more bluff than anything, the contest being bloodless. The male displaying most actively or with the larger 'sail' usually intimidates his rival. In courtship the male comes over to the female with all sails set and with fins quivering takes up position across her path. At the same time he displays colours which, though always present, are shown on these occasions only.

Food

The mollies are mainly vegetarian but also take small amounts of animal food, such as water fleas and mosquito larvae.

Eggs develop inside female

The mollies' reproductive life is full of unusual events. The male's anal fin is modified to form a gonopodium with which he puts sperm into the female's oviduct where the young develop and are subsequently born alive. Several weeks pass between fertilisation and birth, the length of time depending mainly on temperature. The young lie curled head to tail in the oviduct and are born one or two at a time.

Permanently fatherless

There is a natural tendency in mollies towards the production of the black pigment, melanin, and occasionally all black 'sports' are produced. The aquarist takes advantage of this to breed black mollies. The black sports are obtained mainly from the sail-

Female black molly on the right of the picture is pursued by males. The male anal fin is modified to form a gonopodium with which he puts sperm into the female's oviduct. The anal fin of the female is fully developed. The large sail-like dorsal fin is used in aggressive and courtship displays.

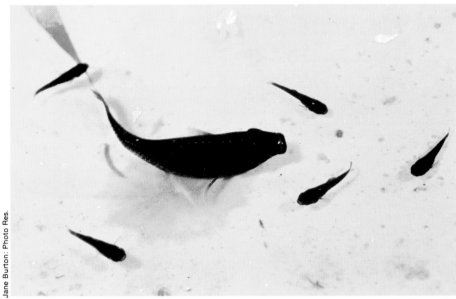

Jane Burton: Photo Res.

△ *Mother with young mollies, which developed curled head to tail in the female's oviduct. (Lifesize).*

▽ *Black mollies have been selectively bred by fish fanciers from several molly species.*

Jane Burton: Photo Res.

fin *Mollienisia latipinna*, less often from the sail-bearer *M. velifera* and occasionally from the wedge-face *M. sphenops*. When the young blacks are born they may be light or dark in colour. Most of them become light in a few weeks and only when about 1 in. long do they begin to show black spots. Six months from birth some will have become all black. Others may not become black for 2 years, and some never do. One strain, the 'permablack', however, is born black and remains so.

The black mollies themselves are attractive to the eye and so have become favourites of the dilettante aquarist. To the more discerning, they are even more attractive, for their genetical peculiarities. This is true of all the mollies. One is *M. formosa* living in the rivers of Texas and Mexico.

M. formosa is a natural hybrid resulting from a cross between *M. latipinna* and *M. sphenops*. The hybrid has characters intermediate between those of the two parents and this intermediate form is perpetuated in a quite unusual way. The hybrids are nearly all females, and they produce only female offspring. They cannot do so, however, unless a male *M. latipinna* or *M. sphenops* is present. Mating then occurs and presumably the sperms enter the ova but they are rejected, so that what the sperms have done is to set in motion all those things which normally result from the fertilisation of an ovum, while contributing nothing to the offspring.

So, when a *formosa* female mates with a *latipinna* male, all the progeny look like the mother in every respect. When a *formosa* female mates with a *sphenops* male all the progeny, again, look like the mother. In fact, the same is true if a *formosa* female mates with the male of any of the species of *Mollienisia*. Moreover, very rarely, perhaps once in every 10 000, a male *formosa* is born. Presumably it can mate, but so far there is no evidence as to whether he contributes anything to the offspring.

This extraordinary state of affairs can be tested merely by looking at populations of *formosa*. Mother and offspring look alike, behave alike, and have the same internal anatomy. That they are truly alike can be tested by transplanting tissues.

We are familiar now with the surgical operations of heart and kidney transplants, the early attempts at which were mainly unsuccessful. This was because the patients' bodies rejected the alien tissues. We can be fairly certain that a heart transplant would be wholly successful if performed between identical twins, because experiments have shown that other tissue grafts between identical twins are always successful. Many experiments have been carried out on mollies, transplanting fins, heart and spleen from daughter to mother and between the progeny of a single mother, and there is never any rejection.

class	**Osteichthyes**
order	**Atheriniformes**
family	**Poeciliidae**
genus & species	**Mollienisia latipinna** *sail-fin* **M. formosa** *Amazon molly* *others*

△ *Black widow, sitting on its web with the feet touching the silken strands, waits for a victim (× 6).*

▽ *The spider begins to wrap and secure its victim by using quantities of silk from spinnerets (× 18).*

▽ *Often it is only at this stage that the victim is stabbed with the fangs and paralysed, then the back legs are skilfully used to enshroud almost completely the ant victim in the viscid silk (× 6).*

Black widow

This is a species of spider with a number of subspecies widely distributed over the warmer parts of the world. The North American subspecies is especially noted for its powerful venom, a reputation which is not fully justified. The female is about ½ in. long, a shiny velvety black with a red hour-glass mark on the underside of her almost spherical abdomen. The male is much smaller. The size and colour of the female has led to the alternative names which include shoe button spider, red mark, red back, jockey and also hour-glass spider. The more familiar name of black widow is based on her colour and on the reputation she has for eating her mate as soon as he has fertilised her. It seems possible that the strength of the venom varies with the subspecies and the one inhabiting the southern United States seems to be the worst.

Painful but not fatal

The black widow spins a coarse irregularly designed web which often has a short funnel of silk, usually in the more elevated area. The male spins a similarly textured web but much smaller. Cool dark places are chosen, in cellars, outbuildings, ruined or abandoned houses, under doorsteps and porches, beneath floorboards or in piles of rubbish. Among the outbuildings must be included the primitive latrine where, it seems, most human victims have been attacked. Proportionately with the large numbers in which it exists the number of people who fall victim is surprisingly small. The known cases of injury or death in the United States for the 217 years between 1726 and 1943 are 1 291, only 55 of which are known to have been fatal. That is, one death in every 4 years and half a dozen injuries per year. Moreover, the evidence suggests that a high percentage of injuries have been sustained in rural areas where the plumbing is primitive, and even there the victims are mainly children or elderly or unwell people. Above all there seems a strong suggestion that when death does occur shock is a contributory factor if not the sole cause. Nevertheless, the non-fatal consequences are unpleasant enough. The poison is a neurotoxin which attacks the nerves to cause severe pain, muscular cramp, paralysis and hypertension. Fortunately the spider itself is retiring and more concerned with avoiding people than with attacking them. And only the females are troublesome as the male is too small to have enough venom to have any significant effect on humans.

With the exception of one family all spiders have poison glands. These lie in the cephalothorax, the smaller and front portion of the two parts that make up a spider's body, and the poison passes through slender ducts to the fangs. In all but a few spiders, the black widow being one, the venom is effective only against small animals such as insects. It is introduced into their bodies by a stabbing action rather than a bite since no jaw mechanism is involved, the mouthparts of a spider being capable only of sucking.

Paralysed victim enshrouded in silk

As with other web-weaving spiders the black widow sits on the web with her feet touching the silken strands. When an insect flies into the web and starts to struggle the vibrations are detected through the feet of the spider who immediately runs out, and by skilfully using her rear legs and quantities of the viscid silk from the spinnerets, quickly binds and secures it. Often it is only at this stage that the victim is stabbed with the fangs and paralysed, subsequently to be almost completely enshrouded in silk. Meanwhile a drop or two of saliva containing a protein-splitting ferment is exuded from the spider's mouthparts into the insect's body, the contents of which are therefore digested externally. This takes an hour or two, at the end of which the spider, by using its muscular stomach as a pump, sucks out the 'soup', leaving behind only the husk of its prey. This the spider finally cuts away and lets fall to the ground.

Pedipalp sperm reservoir

When adult, the male seeks a mate but before doing so he spins a very tiny web, rubs his abdomen against this and ejects on to it a drop of seminal fluid. This he then takes up in his pedipalps, a pair of specially adapted appendages situated near the mouth and resembling short legs. In mating the male merely transfers the sperm from the reservoir in the pedipalp to the female's body, only one mating being necessary for several bouts of egg-laying, since the female stores the sperm and uses it over a period, often of months. The eggs are laid in silken cocoons and the spiderlings hatching from them are, apart from colour, more or less replicas of the parents and independent from the start.

Self imposed widows

Almost everyone believes that the female spider invariably eats her spouse after mating. Even some of those who study spiders join in the chorus possibly after having occasionally seen this happen. This, it is said, is the reason for naming this most venomous spider the black widow. Certainly few people have ever sat down and watched hundreds of spiders mating to see whether the male is invariably eaten. Therefore this idea that the female always eats her spouse is based on this act of cannibalism being occasionally seen. There is, however, a more reasonable explanation. For example, we are told by one expert after another that when the male spider has transferred his sperm to a female he replenishes the reservoir in his pedipalps and will do so several times. This is consistent with the accepted and oft-repeated statement, that male spiders are polygamous—a polygamous male obviously cannot meet his death at each mating. The more likely explanation, and one consistent with the facts, is that after several matings the male becomes enfeebled, is indeed moribund, and then it is that the female devours him, as she would any similar small animal that came her way.

It is a fact that in the insect house at the London Zoo where black widows have been bred in large numbers for many years, individual male spiders have often been mated many times.

phylum	**Arthropoda**
class	**Arachnida**
order	**Araneae**
family	**Theridiidae**
genus & species	***Latrodectus mactans***

Black widow with her completed cocoon. On hatching the spiderlings, apart from colours, are more or less replicas of the parents and independent from the start. The name widow comes from the belief that the female eats the male after mating. This does happen, but only occasionally.

David Hughes

Blenny

The blennies, together with the related blenny-like fishes, are almost as numerous as the stars in the heavens. There are nearly a score of families and most of these contain numerous species of mainly small shallow water fishes living in tropical and temperate seas. They can readily be found on rocky shores when the tide is out, under stones or seaweed, especially in rock pools. They have elongated bodies, and are usually less than 6 in. long. The pelvic fins are absent or very small and attached under the throat, and the dorsal fin extends from the back of the head almost to the tail or is even continuous with it.

Research on fish behaviour

The casual naturalist searching the shore sees the blenny only as a small fish that darts across a rock pool, when a stone is lifted, and vanishes under another stone. The ease with which blennies can be found and caught has made them favourites for study in aquaria. This has shed light on their behaviour in relation to tides and on their social hierarchies.

As long ago as 1877, a Mr Ross of Topsham, in Devon, kept a shanny, a species of blenny, in a glass tank filled with sea water. He noticed the fish became restless as the time of high tide approached. When he put a large stone in the tank, with its top clear of water, the shanny would leave the water to lie on the rock when the time for low tide arrived. It would drop back into the water at high tide. Ross found, during the many months he had it, that the shanny always knew the state of the tide.

There are places, the Mediterranean being one, where the tides are feeble or non-existent. The blennies living there have no need for a biological clock, and it has been found by experiments similar to those made by Ross, but differing in that the blennies could not leave the water, that after a while the fishes behaved as if they were living in a tideless zone.

With such small fishes living on a rocky or stony bottom observation of their behaviour once the tide is in is almost impossible. It can, however, be pieced together by watching them in aquaria that approach as nearly as possible the natural state. From such studies it is clear that once they are covered with water by the returning tide they become fully active. One of their activities, naturally, is feeding, but much time is spent in chasing one another.

Each digs a shelter under a stone or rock, excavating the sand by wriggling its body. It may make several such shelters and it alternately comes out to feed and darts back to shelter. There is, however, no holding of territories with fixed boundaries which birds and other animals are known to do. A blenny moves about over what is called its home range. It has an individual distance and it grows uneasy should another blenny intrude within that distance. Then we see that one blenny will be dominant, another will be subordinate. Two coming

near each other will show fight, butting with the head or biting, or merely raising their fins in a display of force. The dominant individual always prevails, the subordinate giving way and retreating.

Similarly, if a subordinate is in a shelter and a dominant enters the subordinate will leave it. The tables are reversed when a subordinate enters the shelter of a dominant. It is driven out. Blennies also have favourite resting places on rocks, and these are determined by this same kind of 'peck order', the boss blenny driving the others away.

The scale of dominance, which can be seen even in young blennies, is largely determined by size, and the more nearly two blennies are matched for size the more likely is a fight to develop. The most this amounts to is that one may bite the other, inflicting only superficial wounds. Something of this kind was demonstrated by two American scientists with blennies in an aquarium, that became tame enough to swim across for food. If a cupped hand was lowered into the water one of the blennies would come to rest in the hand. Soon it would be driven out by one of the others nibbling its tail. At times a continuous procession would result, each taking a turn to lie in the hand and then being driven out by the next.

In aquaria blennies are alert and they look intelligent. Several experimenters have shown that blennies can be readily taught, to come for food at certain places, even to take food off particular hooks, or to wait at other places to be fed. This is done by what is called reward and punishment, or, to use the terms preferred by scientists, 'positive and negative reinforcement'. One scientist showed that blennies could be trained to tell apart objects by their colours, brightness, shape and size, numbers and position. For example, they could be taught

to tell the difference between such letters as U and E, W and L, and to recognize two or more letters in a group.

One feature of the behaviour which may contribute to the appearance of intelligence, if not to an actual intelligence, is the ability to move the eyes independently. Certainly this gives an air of watchfulness, but this may be no more than a normal requirement for fishes living in shallow water with many enemies.

Browses on barnacles

Little is known precisely about the food of blennies in the natural state. It is usually said that they are carnivorous or omnivorous. In aquaria they will eat bits of meat, worms and small crustaceans swimming near the surface. From this we can presume their diet is wide. A shanny in an aquarium will even browse acorn barnacles, crushing the strong shells with its teeth.

Father guards the eggs

Blennies usually lay eggs but at least one bears living young and is called the viviparous blenny. The eggs are oval or pear shaped, and are laid, as a rule, in empty mollusc shells, in crevices in rocks, in empty bottles lying on the bottom. One was even seen to lay eggs in a large hollow beef bone. They are attached to the inner surfaces of such objects and guarded by the male, rarely by both parents, who by movements of his tail keeps the water around the eggs moving to oxygenate them. Some of the blennies which live in Caribbean waters, and are called kelpfishes, lay their eggs inside sponges. The young fishes stay for a while inside the sponge, feeding on small plankton brought in by the currents of water drawn in by the sponge (see p 305).

The viviparous blenny *Zoarces viviparus* is not a true blenny but is one of the blenny-

Portrait of the common blenny. Living in shallow waters blennies are vulnerable to many enemies. Independent movement of the eyes gives the blenny a good wide view, so it sees if danger threatens.

Jane Burton: Photo Res.

373

DP Wilson

Male butterfly blenny guards eggs laid in a disused milk bottle. He moves his tail to keep the water round the eggs moving to oxygenate them.

ES Hobson

Blenny peering out from its shelter. Each blenny digs a shelter, or often several, under a rock or stone, excavating sand by wriggling its body.

like fishes referred to in the introduction. Also known as the eelpout, it belongs to the family Zoarcidae, most of whose members are viviparous. The eggs hatch within the female's body about 3 weeks after fertilisation but the babies are not born until 4 months later. Each is 1½ in. long when born, and a single female 7−8 in. long may give birth to 20−40 at a time. The largest females may give birth to as many as 300 at a time.

The shanny can live as long as 4 years and other blennies probably have a similar life-span.

Vulnerable at low tide

Blennies are probably more vulnerable at low tide, and more especially when breeding, than when covered with water. Gulls will then take them, and so will rats scavenging the shore. Nevertheless, it must be con-

ceded that blennies are well camouflaged by their colours and the mottled patterns on the bodies. Some, like the shanny, can change colour according to their background.

Enlarged gland makes amphibious fish

Blennies, as we have seen, readily survive each period of ebb-tide sheltering under stones or seaweeds. Some carry this further and tend to leave the water for appreciable periods of time. It was some such tendency that caused the original invasion of land by fish ancestors that gave rise to the land vertebrates, including man.

It seems that this was not necessarily due to any impulse or urge to leave the sea to escape competition, the reason usually given, but the result of an enlarged gland.

Fishes, like the blennies, capable of an amphibious existence have a large thyroid gland. Moreover, there is one blenny *Blennius ocellatus* that normally spends its whole life in water, breathing by gills, taking in oxygen dissolved in the water. When injected with an extract of thyroid it takes on an amphibious life and will breathe air (atmospheric oxygen) for as much as 8 hours on end.

class	**Osteichthyes**
order	**Perciformes**
family	**Blenniidae**
genera	***Blennius, Hypsoblennius*** *others*

◁ *A blenny exposed at low tide is vulnerable to gulls and rats scavenging on the shore. The body colours and mottled patterns give, however, quite effective camouflage.*

▽ *Boss blenny on an empty crab case waiting to drive a small one away as soon as it comes out.*

Jane Burton: Photo Res.

Blesbok herd on open grassland in South Africa.

Blesbok

The early settlers and travellers in South Africa recorded herds of thousands of these animals on the plains, but their slaughter for food, to satisfy big game hunters or to make way for agriculture reduced their numbers to a precarious figure.

Blesbok are small antelopes standing a little over 4 ft at the shoulder and weighing over 150 lb. They are very similar in size and colour to the bontebok antelope. The coat is soft, rufous brown on the back, becoming almost black and very glossy on the rump. Around the base of the tail there is a patch of white but this is not nearly so conspicuous as that of the closely-related bontebok. A white blaze runs from the horns, down between the eyes and spreading out over the muzzle to the nostrils. Between the eyes the blaze becomes constricted and may appear as two blazes with a bar of brown hair separating them. In calves the blaze is black, becoming lighter as they grow older. At the age of one year it is mottled and is white by the time they are mature.

The horns, which are carried by both sexes, are described as lyrate from their lyre-like appearance. Viewed from the front, they bend away from each other then straighten out vertically. At the same time they curve back over the neck. The horns grow to lengths of 18 in. Those of the females are rather more slender than those of the males.

South African habitat

The original range of the blesbok was confused by some writers because of the similarity between the blesbok and the bontebok. This confusion existed especially in the south where the ranges of the two antelopes met. It seems that in the latter part of the 19th century blesbok were to be found from the Northern Karroo, through the Orange Free State and into the high veldt of the Transvaal, around Johannesburg.

This range is now very much limited and many blesbok now live as semi-wild animals on farms. In 1962 counts were made in some parts of South Africa and nearly 9 000 were found in Cape Province, 12 000 in the Orange Free State and 25 000 in the Transvaal. These figures do not approach the numbers of the original populations but with today's protection blesbok are no longer in danger of extinction.

Blesbok prefer rather high, open ground where they associate in mixed herds of males and females, although herds of young bulls may form from those driven out of the main herds by the strongest bulls.

Unlike some of its relatives, such as the klipspringer (p. 1379) and beira antelope (p. 330), the blesbok is not good at leaping. At the farms where it is bred, a fence 4½ ft high is sufficient to keep stock in. It is more necessary to fix strands of wire near the ground to stop blesbok crawling underneath.

Short grass grazers

Blesbok graze on short grass. In this way they do not seriously compete with cattle and on the farms cattle are necessary to remove the long grass to allow the blesbok to thrive on the shorter stems. On the other hand, in the dry season blesbok retain their healthy condition far better than cattle.

376

Popperfoto

When water is accessible blesbok will drink at least once a day, but can go without for several days although they become restless and lose their healthy appearance.

Two-month rutting season
During the mating season the herds split up. A male separates a small number of females from the herd and guards them against other males. Rutting starts in April and continues for 2 months. The single calves are born from November to February after a gestation of some $7\frac{1}{2}$ months. Females are sexually mature at 18 months, males later.

Jackals are main enemy
The lion and the leopard must have been important predators at one time but now most blesbok are semi-domesticated and live on farms far from lion country, jackals are their main predators. Adult blesbok, however, are more than a match for jackals, though some calves may be taken.

Domesticating blesbok
Within recent years there have been many projects in Africa to farm wild animals.

There are many reasons for preferring the wild hoofed animals to domestic cattle, sheep or goats. The main one is that the wild animals belong to the country and are adapted to live there. They do not suffer from the diseases that trouble imported stock and they are able to utilise the rough herbage better than domesticated animals from temperate regions that need high-quality pasture to survive. They are also less dependent on a good water supply. Furthermore, it has been shown recently that antelopes yield a higher proportion of meat protein per unit of body size than cattle. There is less fat on the body, such fat as there is differs in composition from that of cattle, and there is evidence that the fat on antelopes is less likely to cause disorders of the heart and circulation.

There are now several ranches in South Africa where blesbok are reared for their meat. In the Transvaal some 1 500 blesbok are harvested per year, yielding about $1 800 (£750), and the value of the carcases is increasing each year. The meat tastes very like beef so that it is quite acceptable even to people who don't like trying new foods.

Usually the blesbok are kept on ranches with cattle although they are not kept together as they fight. Their difference in grazing habits prevents the blesbok from taking the best grazing from the cattle. Keeping blesbok with arable farming has also been tried. The blesbok have been confined to uplands then allowed into maize fields after the harvest to supplement their winter feed with the stubble and spilt grains.

Being able to keep two species of stock animal on the same piece of land is obviously an advantage as the ground will yield extra profit without having to invest in improving its fertility. It may be possible to extend this by introducing browsing animals to feed on shrubs.

class	**Mammalia**
order	**Artiodactyla**
family	**Bovidae**
genus & species	***Damaliscus dorcas phillipsi***

BLOODHOUNDS

The Bloodhound, a British breed, is the oldest and largest of the scent hounds. It is a massive hound, particularly characterized by long ears and loose skin, and has been used for centuries for tracking man, being renowned for its wonderful nose, its tenacity and relentless determination in following its quarry, and its beautiful, deep, belling voice.

The Bloodhound is thought to be a direct descendant of the black St Hubert Hound and the white Talbot Hound, both extinct, which were brought to England with the Norman Conquest and bred with the indigenous hound found in Britain in pre-Christian times, which may have been brought there by the Trojans. They were originally used to discover the whereabouts of deer and to track down wounded game, hunting various quarry in packs. It has been used for 'hunting the clean boot' (tracking human quarry by scent without an artificial drag) for many centuries. It is considered to have a better nose than any other breed of dog. Most of the scent hounds and many gun dogs carry its blood. Particularly noted is the Bloodhound's ability to follow a very cold scent and its perseverance in working out difficult trails. There have been many instances of Bloodhounds finding their quarry after unbelievably long periods, the record for a proven case being nearly 14 days.

Unwarranted reputation
There have been countless stories of Bloodhounds' prowess at mantrailing over the centuries. Indeed, such is its reputation for relentlessly pursuing its quarry that when two Bloodhounds were brought to London to help solve the Jack the Ripper murders, the atrocities ceased, and the crime rate generally in the City fell drastically, until the hounds were returned to their home.

The Bloodhound has acquired an unwarranted reputation for ferocity, probably from tales of Southern penitentiaries and plantations, where so-called Bloodhounds were used to trail escaped convicts and slaves. These dogs were trained to tree their quarry and were extremely savage, but few if any were real Bloodhounds.

The present day Bloodhound throughout the world is descended from stock exported from Great Britain, where, during the Second World War, numbers sank dangerously low, and were increased by the use of an outcross to the Dumfriesshire hound (a large black and tan hound owing much of its breeding to the Bloodhound, very similar in appearance to the Coonhound) and stud dogs imported from the USA and Canada. Outcrosses have been used throughout the centuries to maintain the health, stamina and longevity of this numerically small breed.

Strong tracking instinct
To this day the Bloodhound tracks man. With the increasing urbanization in its country of origin, it is less frequently called out for police work, the constabulary preferring to use their own general purpose dogs, although it is freely admitted that as a tracker dog the Bloodhound stands supreme.

However, on the Continent, in the USA, Canada, Israel and in other countries, the Bloodhound is still used for serious mantrailing with great success. The Bloodhound's tracking instinct is highly developed, the training of a puppy being largely to encourage this instinct and discipline any tendency to deviate from the proper scent. Very young puppies who can hardly walk will use their noses as other animals would use their eyes. As soon as they are physically strong enough they thoroughly enjoy a game of hide and seek, and this develops as they grow older, until they can follow trails of several miles, hours after the track has been laid. The Bloodhound is renowned for its determination in following the scent of one person so that, whilst working, it is difficult to stop. It is the only breed of dog whose evidence is accepted in a court of law.

Slow maturers
Known as Nature's Gentleman, the Bloodhound is characterized by solemnity, wisdom and power, although it has a well developed sense of humour. It is of an amiable, noble disposition, seldom given to fighting, but can be formidable if roused. This breed matures slowly, physically and mentally, and should be treated with affection combined with firmness or it can become unmanageable. Whilst showing deep loyalty to those it considers friends, it is reserved with strangers and may be timid in unusual surroundings. Its guarding instincts are strong and a person is foolhardy who enters unannounced a Bloodhound's home.

The Bloodhound's solemn appearance belies its playful disposition. Bloodhounds are very sensitive and require gentle, considerate handling.

Blowfly

These are the bluebottles and greenbottles that are so unpopular in the kitchen. Their form is very similar to that of the housefly, differing mainly in microscopic features, but they are generally larger and their bodies have a metallic blue or green sheen.

The name blowfly refers to their habit of laying eggs in meat, 'fly-blown' meat being decaying meat with the larvae, or maggots, of flies in it. Blown, in this context, has nothing to do with the usual meaning. It comes from an Old English usage. A fly depositing its eggs was said to be blowing.

Proboscis searches for putrefying food

Blowflies feed on the liquids of putrefying food and carrion or on nectar obtained from flowers. They suck these fluids up a flexible tube, or proboscis, which is formed from their mouth parts. There are organs of taste both on the tip of the proboscis and on the tarsi, or feet. If the fly walks across something edible, it will automatically feed. Experiments have shown that if a blowfly is gently lowered onto a pad impregnated with sugar solution, its proboscis uncoils and starts probing for food as soon as its legs touch the pad.

When a blowfly finds some food it begins searching in circles, and the more food it finds, the tighter becomes its circling. This is an instinctive set piece of behaviour, but it leads the blowfly to exploit food supplies to the best advantage. If food is scarce the fly searches over a wide area, but when it finds a good source it stays there to feed.

Life cycle on carrion

The life cycle of blowflies is the same as that of most flies. Eggs are laid on suitable food, the larvae or maggots live on this food, pupate and emerge about a fortnight later as shortlived adults. Blowflies are of interest because their life histories are varied, with some species laying their eggs in strange places.

The female blowfly lays up to 600 eggs on carrion, where there is exposed flesh from a wound or in the eye-sockets, mouth and other body openings of animals. Some species are considered pests by sheep farmers as they lay their eggs in open sores and in the genital openings of ewes. They are also a serious household pest. The familiar bluebottle buzzing heavily around the kitchen or larder is probably a female blowfly in search of meat on which to lay her eggs. The coolness and darkness of a larder that deter other species of fly are no obstacle to blowflies, which seem able to get to meat despite precautions taken by the housewife. Sometimes blowflies are ovoviviparous. If egg-laying is delayed for some reason, lack of a suitable laying place perhaps, the eggs are retained in the female's body, where they hatch out and duly leave her body as larvae, or maggots.

Normally, the eggs take a day to hatch and the larvae live for a week before pupating, when $\frac{3}{4}$ in. long. Blowfly larvae are the 'gentles' of the fisherman, forming a good

Jane Burton: Photo Res.

△ *Bluebottles feeding and searching for sites to lay eggs on the head of a dead snake.*
▽ *Blowfly with its feeding tube, the proboscis, extended sucking up nectar from the flower head.*

▽ *Anatomy of the proboscis of the blowfly. Liquid food is collected into the numerous food canals and passed into the central canal, which leads to the alimentary canal.*

Stephen Dalton: NHPA

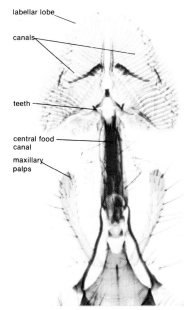

labellar lobe

canals

teeth

central food canal

maxillary palps

Gene Cox

bait for many kinds of coarse fish. There are even 'gentle farms' where blowfly larvae are bred in immense numbers.

The maggots are rather different from the caterpillars of butterflies and moths or the larvae of bugs like aphids (see p. 69) and assassin bugs (see p. 98). They are little more than fleshy bags that eat and breathe. They have no legs and can move only by wriggling. However, the maggots have little need to move as they are surrounded by food, which is being liquefied by bacteria and by the larva's enzymes, which are poured onto the food.

Before pupating, the larvae wriggle away from the flesh on which they have been feeding. The skin of the larva forms the pupa case and within it the body is almost completely broken down and rebuilt in the adult form. This takes about a week, and the adult forces its way out of the pupa case by sucking in air and doubling its size, which splits the case open.

Apart from the blowflies that lay their eggs in rotting meat or in open wounds, there are some that lay their eggs on healthy animals. One species, *Lucilia bufonivora*, lays its eggs on the eyes and in the nostrils of toads and frogs. The maggots penetrate the body and feed on the living tissues. The larvae of some species live in earthworms. The eggs of *Pollenia rudis* are laid in the earth in autumn and larvae invade the bodies of earthworms and hibernate. In the spring they move along their hosts' bodies devouring their tissues.

Wounds heal quickly

During the First World War doctors working in the hospitals behind the entrenched armies were surprised to find that the wounds of soldiers that had been un-attended for several days and were in-fested with maggots healed quickly, and often more quickly than wounds that had received immediate attention. Blowflies have a well-founded reputation of spreading infection, by picking up bacteria and spreading them by walking over food or regurgi-tating them in their saliva. It was surprising, then, that those unattended wounds, which probably would have become infected with-out any maggots present, healed so rapidly. The doctors found that the maggots were, in fact, eating away the suppurating flesh so that the suppuration did not spread and the flesh could heal.

This was well before the days of penicillin and other drugs, at a time when relatively slight wounds could become fatal, especi-ally in the primitive conditions near a battle-field. Consequently maggots were specially bred in sterile conditions and put into sup-purating wounds. Unpleasant as this may seem, it is certainly better than having an in-fected wound that can lead to death.

class	**Insecta**
order	**Diptera**
family	**Calliphoridae**
genera	***Calliphora***
	Lucilia
	Pollenia
	others

Blowfly life cycle

Blowfly eggs are laid among the hairs of a dead mammal, which serves as food for the larvae or maggots (1). The female blowfly can lay up to 600 eggs, usually on carrion, but also on exposed flesh wounds or on other body openings of animals. Maggots, hatching from the eggs usually within a day, are little more than fleshy bags which eat and breathe (2). They feed and grow for a week, pupating when ¾ in. long. Before pupating, the larvae wriggle away from the flesh on which they have been feeding. The skin of the larva forms the pupa case (3) and within it the body is completely broken down and rebuilt. In about a week the adult forces its way out of the pupal case by sucking in air and doubling its size which splits the cap of the case open (4). The adult blowfly, a bluebottle or greenbottle, climbs out to live for about 2 weeks (5).

Series by Stephen Dalton: NHPA

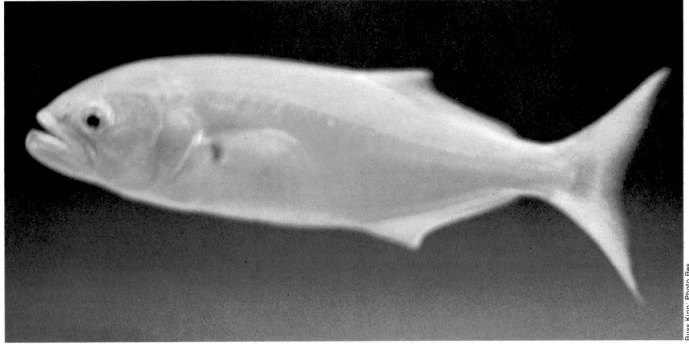

The swift-moving bluefish swims in large shoals and attacks other fishes with unparalleled ferocity. It is caught commercially and for sport.

Bluefish

The bluefish is remarkable for its voracity and has long been known as an ocean killer. There is a single species occupying a family to itself. The bluefish, bass-like and usually about 15 in. long, lives in schools in tropical and subtropical waters, except for the central and eastern Pacific. Its range seems to be extending. Since 1945, for example, it has become familiar to the fishermen of Tuscany who believe it followed American ships there in the Second World War, and to whom it is known as the American fish. Bluish or greenish in colour with a black blotch at the base of each pectoral fin, it has a dorsal fin in two parts, the spinous portion in front being the smaller. In summer they may come into estuaries when seasonally abundant offshore.

Ferocity unparalleled

Bluefish are swift-moving fish that appear suddenly in large shoals as much as 4−5 miles long and attack other fishes with almost unparalleled ferocity. Little is known of their migrations, except that they may travel considerable distances, but it is believed there may be regional races. Also they may winter in deep water, between perhaps 300−600 ft, as bluefish have been caught in trawls at these depths in winter.

Animated chopping machines

Other fishes of all kinds are attacked, and off the Atlantic coast of North America menhaden *Brevortia tyrannus* especially are preyed upon. A feature of bluefish is that they behave like animated chopping machines, cutting fishes even as large as themselves to pieces and continuing to do so until satiated. The trail of a shoal is then marked by fragments of fish and blood, often with dead fish having only a portion bitten away. It has been estimated that a thousand million bluefish may occur annually in the western Atlantic in summer. Allowing a ration of ten fish a day for each bluefish, this amounts to 1 200 000 000 000 fishes killed in a single season. These figures may be slightly exaggerated but they epitomize the habits of bluefish, which, even when only a fraction of an inch, are a menace to other fishes.

40 million pounds caught annually

There are no known enemies other than man, who catches bluefish for its palatable flesh. Commercial fisheries in the United States account for 4 million pounds weight annually, and sports fishermen catch over ten times this amount.

Bluefish rising to fisherman's bait.

Life history studied in the laboratory

Spawning is in June to August, the eggs, 1¼ mm diameter, are probably laid well out to sea. These hatch 44−46 hours later, the newly-hatched fish being about $\frac{1}{10}$ in. long. At first, the jaws and gills are non-functional, the eyes are without pigment and there are no pectoral fins, the young fish being dependent on its yolk sac for a supply of food. At a year old it will have grown to 16 in., at 2 years to 20 in., at 3 years to 28 in., with weights of 1, 2 and 4 lb respectively. The record fish caught on a line weighed 24 lb 3 oz and measured 41 in. North African bluefish are said to reach 45 lb.

The most detailed account of the development of the eggs is that given by LP Salekhova, from study of bluefish taken in the Black Sea and kept in aquaria. The eggs were transparent and at 25 hours after fertilisation the chief organs had been formed in the embryo. At 37 hours the heart began to beat. After that the embryo turned from time to time during the remaining 7−9 hours before hatching.

Fish makes history

In 1871 Spencer Fullerton Baird was invited to investigate a supposed decline in the New England commercial shore fisheries. Hook and line fishermen blamed trap fishermen, who in turned blamed the bluefish. Baird, in his report, recommended controls for trap-fishing but included a blistering attack on the iniquities of the bluefish. It was he who suggested the astronomical figures given above under food. Baird's Commission, the United States Commission for Fish and Fisheries, was still in being when he died, in 1887. He was still Fish Commissioner, with a permanent laboratory at Wood's Hole, on Cape Cod, the oldest marine laboratory in North America. Moreover, the US Fish and Wildlife Service, now a tremendous organisation, can trace its beginnings to Baird's Fish Commission and the bluefish!

class	**Osteichthyes**
order	**Perciformes**
family	**Pomatomidae**
genus & species	***Pomatomus saltatrix***

Blues

A cosmopolitan group of butterflies, containing several hundred species belonging to the same family as the coppers and hairstreaks. The Arctic blue ranges from Greenland across Scandinavia and Siberia to Alaska. The pigmy blue of the southern part of North America is the smallest of butterflies with a wing spread of ½ in. None of the blues is large and they are generally rather fragile. Eight species are found in the British Isles, with three species coming to Britain only as migrants. The mazarine blue bred in Dorset during the 19th century but now appears only as a summer visitor. The long-tailed and short-tailed blues, which have short 'tails' on the hind wings so that they resemble hairstreaks, are rare summer visitors to Britain, but are commonly found elsewhere in Europe, and also in Africa.

Although many species are blue in colour, some are whitish and brown, and a great many females are wholly brown. The undersides of the wings, usually white or brown in contrast with the uppersides, are often marked with orange or black spots. The brown argus of Europe is a brown butterfly that does, in fact, belong to the blues.

Cannibal caterpillar

Eggs are usually laid singly on the leaves, or tucked into the flowers of plants. Some blues will lay eggs on a variety of plants whereas others are restricted to one kind of plant. Vetches, trefoils and gorse are often used. The holly blue lays its eggs on holly, dogwood, buckthorn and other shrubs, and the eggs lie dormant over winter, hatching out in April.

When small, the caterpillars eat the outer layers of the leaves or flowers, but later they are able to chew right through them or burrow down into the flowerheads. Often the caterpillars are cannibals, devouring their fellows until only one is left on each flower head or leaf.

The caterpillars of the small blue and long-tailed blue hibernate. The small blue caterpillar retires as early as July. Having fed on the growing seed pods of the kidney vetch, it makes a shelter of a few flowers bound together with silk and hides there until the following spring, looking very much like the withered flowers around it.

The pupa is formed usually on a leaf or stem, the caterpillar first anchoring itself by a band of silk. Some emerge as adults in a few weeks, others remain in the pupal stage for the winter.

In many parts of the world, caterpillars of blues have glands on the abdomen which secrete a sugary fluid called honeydew. This is rather like the honeydew of aphides (see page 167) and it also attracts the attentions of ants which stimulate the secretion by caressing the caterpillars with their antennae and legs. The presence of ants around the

△ *Common blues mating, the bluish male at the top. The adult life is about 20 days (3 × lifesize).*

△ *Large blue single egg (45 × lifesize).*

△ *Large blue young caterpillar (24 × lifesize).*

▽ *Large blue caterpillar amongst an ant colony where it is milked by the ants for its honeydew.*

Beautiful blues

This large group of butterflies, all small in size, are some of the most beautifully coloured butterflies to be seen. In the blues the sexes differ greatly, the females are usually dark sooty brown, the males show the blue colours.

Female chalk hill blue (2½ × lifesize).

Female common blue (2 × lifesize).

Ants sell their children for honeydew

The silver-studded blue shows the lengths to which ants will go. to get a convenient supply of honeydew, but the large blue enters into an even closer association with them. In return for supplying them with honeydew, the ants allow the large blue

from the ants' usual behaviour, because normally they jealously guard their offspring, killing any intruder. But it seems that the honeydew is so esteemed by the ants that they are willing to sacrifice some of their larvae. Moreover, the ants sometimes bring so many caterpillars into the nest that in the end the ant colony dies out.

Six weeks after being brought into the nest the caterpillar, having grown rapidly, becomes fleshy, white and grub-like. In the winter it hibernates, then completes its growth the next spring and pupates in May. Three weeks later, it emerges as an adult butterfly and leaves the nest.

class	Insecta
order	Lepidoptera
family	Lycaenidae
sub-family	Lycaeninae
genera & species	*Cupido* species
	Plebejus species
	Aricia species
	Polyommatus species
	Lysandra coridon chalk hill
	Lycaena species
	Maculinea species
	Celastrina species

Female adonis blue butterfly (4 × lifesize).

Holly blue (3¼ × lifesize).

caterpillars no doubt protects them from predators, but the links between ant and caterpillar are closer. The caterpillars of some species of blue, such as the chalk hill, do not flourish unless there are ants present to milk them. Ants have been seen carrying caterpillars of this species and the silver-studded blue to the vicinity of their nests, placing them on the correct food plant.

caterpillars to prey on their own larvae. In fact, the butterfly seems to have become parasitic on the ant and cannot survive without it.

After its second moult the caterpillar leaves the thyme where it has been feeding and becomes carnivorous, crawling across the ground looking for insects to eat. Eventually the wandering caterpillar is found by an ant, which walks round it then begins to caress it and drinks the honeydew. Then the caterpillar hunches itself up. This is the signal for the ant to pick it up with its jaws and carry it back to the nest.

The caterpillar is carried to an underground chamber where it stays for nearly a year. Here it settles down amongst the ant larvae, preying on them, and from time to time one of the worker ants visits the caterpillar to milk it. This is a departure

Male silver-studded blue.

383

Blue whale

The largest animals that have ever lived, the blue whales can grow to 100 ft long and weigh as much as 135 tons, the equivalent of 30 elephants or 1 600 men. The average adult blue whale is 85 ft long, weighing just over 100 tons. Only an aquatic animal could achieve such a vast size, where the water can support the body. Not fish but mammals, they breathe through lungs, they have some hair, they are viviparous (bear live young) and suckle their offspring. They evolved over 100 million years ago from primitive land mammals, to become adapted to an aquatic life. Their nearest relatives belong to the ungulates (hoofed mammals). Adult whales show no traces of external hind limbs, although there are internal vestiges of them. The nostrils have migrated to the top of the head and are commonly called the whale's blowhole. In the very young embryos the nostrils are in the normal mammalian position.

Blue whales belong to the group of baleen whales or Mysticeti. Instead of teeth they have two sets of whalebone plates, or baleen, made from modified hair, hanging from the roof of the mouth and looking like a sort of internal moustache. This is why they are called Mysticeti, derived from the Greek mystax *meaning moustache.*

The blue whale is also known as the sulphur-bottom whale, a name which refers to a yellowish film of microscopic plants, called diatoms, which is sometimes found on the underside of blue whales. Normally they are slate-blue except on the tips of the flippers.

Arctic and Antarctic distribution

During the summer blue whales live in the Antarctic and Arctic seas, mainly in areas of floating ice. In the winter they migrate into warmer seas where the calves are born. Their movements are dependent largely on the availability of food. In the polar seas there is a vast harvest of small marine creatures but these tend to occur in patches, and by plotting the patches on maps whalers are able to ascertain where they are likely to find the most whales.

Blue whales are usually solitary or associate in small groups only, but sometimes schools of 40–50 have been seen in the winter when several small groups have combined. Like many other kinds of whales, blue whales come to the assistance of their fellows in distress. Where whalers sight two blue whales they know that it is best to shoot the female first because the male will not desert her, and so can be caught easily. On the other hand, the female will desert the harpooned male and so be lost to the whalers.

Whale dives usually last for seven or eight minutes, but blue whales can stay down longer. Their normal speed is 8–10 knots with speeds of up to 18 during sprints. Their power is shown by stories of harpooned whales towing catcher boats.

Fine food filtered for giants

The rows of whalebone plates in the mouths of baleen whales act as sieves, straining off their food of small marine animals. The bulk of the whales' food is a 2 in. shrimp-like animal called krill. To collect krill, a whale opens its mouth and sucks in water. The folds under the jaw and throat of baleen whales allow the floor of the mouth to drop down so a large volume of water can enter. The mouth is then shut and the tongue raised, forcing water out through the baleen plates. Each plate is triangular, broad at the top and tapering to a point at the bottom. They are set $\frac{1}{2}$ in. apart and the inside edge is frayed so that the tough hairs, from which baleen is made up, form a dense mat on which the krill is caught, to be pushed to the back of the mouth by the tongue and swallowed.

The krill exist in the largest concentrations at the surface of the sea, usually within the top 30 ft, so the blue whales do not often have to dive very deep. Krill are also concentrated into certain areas by currents and temperature differences. They are densest in the sea around South Georgia where water coming through the Drake Passage mixes with water coming up from the Weddell Sea. Whales are therefore numerous around South Georgia.

To supply energy to their huge bodies blue whales must be voracious eaters. When cut open in the whaling factories their stomachs are regularly found to be crammed full of krill. One 80 ft individual had 2 tons of krill in its stomach. Occasionally a larger animal, such as a penguin, is found in a whale's stomach, having been engulfed while itself feeding on krill. How the whales find krill in sufficient quantities is rather a mystery. It is known that whales have an echo-location system similar to the asdic or sonar used for hunting submarines. Even with our advanced electronics, however, no system has been built sensitive enough to detect krill.

Calf huge at birth

Female blue whales have their first calf when about five years old, when they measure 70–80 ft long. Mating takes place from May to June and the single calf is born nearly 11 months later when the mother has migrated into warmer water. This is necessary because the calf is born without the insulating layer of blubber to keep it warm. There is, however, less food in the warmer waters and the mother has to draw on the reserves of food built up while feeding in the Antarctic seas.

The calf is 24 ft long when born and doubles in length by the time it is weaned at the age of 7 months. By this time the whales will have returned to the Antarctic where food is plentiful, so the calf will find it relatively easy to learn to feed. As the female does not mate while she has a calf with her, she breeds only once in every two years.

Blue whales threatened by man

Killer whales occasionally band together to attack blue whales, usually picking on young ones. They viciously tear chunks out of the blue whales' bodies, especially from the lips and fins or the bottom of the mouth, and

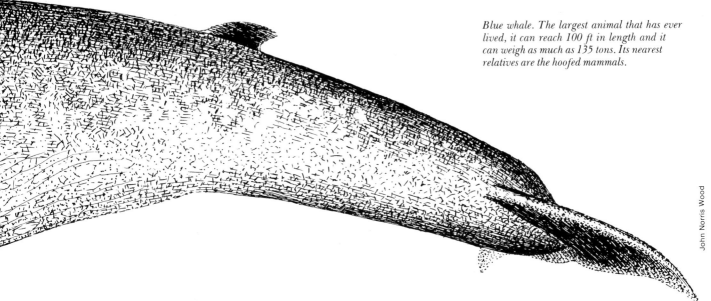

Blue whale. The largest animal that has ever lived, it can reach 100 ft in length and it can weigh as much as 135 tons. Its nearest relatives are the hoofed mammals.

John Norris Wood

even rip out the tongue. Only calves are likely to be killed although adults attacked may die from loss of blood.

Thirty years ago there were an estimated 100 000 blue whales at large in the oceans. Now there are only 2 000 to 6 000. The blue whale had been the main target of the floating whale factories and their fast catcher ships. Not only was a single blue whale such a large prize but, weight for weight, it yielded more blubber than other whales. As a result it was pursued relentlessly, despite warnings from zoologists that too many were being killed. It is only in the last few years that killing blue whales has been banned. Let us hope this ban came in time, for blue whales breed very slowly and there may not be enough left to keep the species from dying out and disappearing altogether.

The wasteful harvest

It is appropriate that in relation to the largest animal that has ever lived we should discuss what is known as the food-pyramid, because the blue whale is a good example of a converter. A familiar example is the domestic cow which can convert grass into flesh for the use of man, who cannot digest grass. Similarly the blue whale converts krill into flesh. The carcase of a whale is a more convenient source of protein and fats than an oceanful of krill. Unfortunately for a world faced with an ever-increasing human population, the process of conversion is very inefficient. To increase its weight by 1 ton, a whale must eat 10 tons of krill. Similarly 1 ton of krill will have eaten 10 tons of minute, floating plants, the phytoplankton, so each ton of whale is eventually nourished by 100 tons of phytoplankton. This represents a loss of 90 per cent at each stage. Only 10 per cent of the energy supplied in an animal's food is used in building up its body, the rest is used in various other processes of life: moving about, keeping warm, reproduction and so on. This low rate of conversion is fairly constant throughout the animal kingdom.

One thing the inefficiency of the food-pyramid shows is the immense abundance of life in the Antarctic seas. At the top of the pyramid stands the whale. Until a few years ago something like 1,200,000 tons of whale carcase were extracted from the sea by the whalers. This represents 12 million tons of krill, a formidable figure but only a fraction of the total of krill when one considers the amount eaten by all the other whales that were not caught, as well as the millions of seabirds and seals, which also feed on krill.

One suggestion put forward is that we should extract food more efficiently from the sea by cutting out one section of the pyramid. Instead of catching whales, we should catch krill, which weight for weight, are ten times more abundant. These could then be directly processed into food for human consumption without the great loss at present sustained in keeping whales alive. Furthermore, it would be possible to regulate the crop, so that we not only obtained food from the Antarctic Ocean but had a healthy population of whales as well. Fishing for krill has been started by the Russians and Japanese and there are fears that if too much is caught the whales, as well as seals and birds, may be robbed of the source of their food.

Antarctic food pyramid shows how 100 tons of plankton are required to ensure the growth of only one ton of a blue whale.

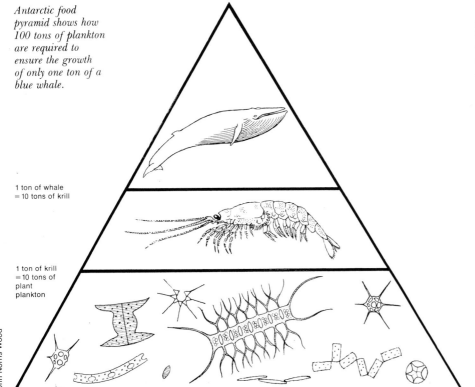

1 ton of whale = 10 tons of krill

1 ton of krill = 10 tons of plant plankton

John Norris Wood

class	**Mammalia**
order	**Cetacea**
family	**Balaenopteridae**
genus & species	***Balaenoptera musculus***

385

Boa

The boa constrictor is one of the stock dangerous animals that the explorers of romantic tales meet. Several snakes of the family Boidae are called boas in ordinary language but none is so well-known as the boa constrictor, although this name has also come to mean any large snake. The boa constrictor is not even the largest of the boa family, being dwarfed by the anaconda (see p. 125). Sizes of most snakes have been exaggerated but there is a reliable record of a boa constrictor 18½ ft long. A 15 ft specimen is considered to be very long.

The boa constrictor is found in the warmest parts of America, from the north of Mexico to Argentina, as well as on the West Indian islands of Trinidad and a few other islands of the Lesser Antilles.

Nocturnal hunter in jungle and desert

Although the boa constrictor is virtually harmless to man it may cause great alarm when found near human habitation. Yet boas are not venomous and, like most animals, they will flee rather than stand and fight. Even if provoked into attacking, most boa constrictors are probably not large enough to kill a man by constriction—that is, throwing a series of strangulatory loops around him. In the event of an attack, the man can easily escape by running, for boas are not swift over the ground. The rosy boa of California, a smaller species, has been recorded as travelling at ¼ mph, with spurts of twice that speed.

The fear inspired by the boa constrictor is shown by a story of how a boa constrictor entered a village in Colombia, presumably in search of food. The villagers fled and asked a white man to seek it out and shoot it. He eventually found it asleep on a bed in one of the houses and duly shot it, but the villagers were still reluctant to return, for, they said, its mate was bound to come looking for it. Unlike its relative the anaconda, which stays near water, the boa constrictor lives in many types of country. In Mexico, it is found in semi-arid parts, on the fringes of deserts, while in tropical America boas live in the dense, wet jungles, but as they seldom enter water they do not compete with the anaconda for food. Furthermore, the boa constrictor spends more time in the trees; the anaconda does little climbing. The boa constrictor is mainly nocturnal but it has been seen hunting during the day.

Crops and plantations are also a haunt of boas and they will come into villages in search of food.

Tall stories

The boa that entered the Colombian village was probably in search of dogs or hens. Apart from this robbing of man, boa constrictors feed on a variety of animals. Terrifying tales of the boa constricting large animals, including man, are common! The majority are very tall stories and the rest grossly exaggerated. Most of the time the boa satisfies its hunger by taking large lizards and birds, such as antbirds. On one occasion a boa was found to have only the tail of a lizard in its stomach. This is interesting evidence of the value of the lizard's ability to shed its tail when caught at its rear end. Only occasionally are largish mammals taken, a 30—40 lb ocelot was found once in a 10 ft specimen. Normally squirrels, opossums, and spiny rats are the mammals eaten.

If boas are such slow movers it is obvious that they cannot chase swiftly moving prey. Rather, they lie in wait or creep up stealthily on an unsuspecting animal. Less prey will be caught by this slow method, but as snakes need food only at long intervals speed is not necessary. When they are inactive they use up little energy and can survive long periods without eating. Even when supplied with plenty of food, some boa constrictors eat very little. One small pet boa ate only 55 white mice in 18 months. This is a very small intake of food compared with that of a flesh-eating mammal, one of a size comparable with the boa being more likely to eat one mouse a day at least.

The boa constrictor's method of killing its prey is, as its name suggests, by constriction. This is not the same as crushing and is fully described for anacondas (see page 41).

The power of a boa constrictor's digestive juices is demonstrated by the boa that ate a porcupine. A few quills were stuck in the mouth, otherwise it had been digested except for some hair and the claws. A series of X-ray photographs were taken of a boa constrictor to show how it digested its prey. A rat was held in the stomach for four days and photographs showed that the bones were gradually being dissolved. During this period the digested products had been released into the intestine to be absorbed.

Breeding

Both males and females of the boas and pythons have a pair of spurs, one either side of the cloaca, the genital and excretory opening. These spurs are the last visible remains of the hind limbs, although these snakes have vestigial pelvic girdles. The male's spurs are longer than the female's and he uses them to stimulate her to mating by scratching her body, especially around the cloaca. Eventually the female raises her tail allowing the male to wrap his tail round her, and mating takes place.

The details of reproduction are not well-known. Mating has been recorded from December to March in Trinidad. Young are born alive with an average length of 20 in. There are usually 20—60 young in each brood. They may double their length in the first year, the rate of growth depending very much on temperature and food supply, and some mature when 2 or 3 years old.

Jungle racer relishes boas

When young, boas have many enemies amongst flesh-eating animals, but as they grow larger fewer of these are able to tackle them. A jungle racer, a notorious snake-eating snake, has been recorded as killing a young boa constrictor.

The boa's reaction to danger is either to

△ *Emerald tree boa anchored to the branch by its prehensile tail, waiting for a bird or small mammal to come within striking range.*

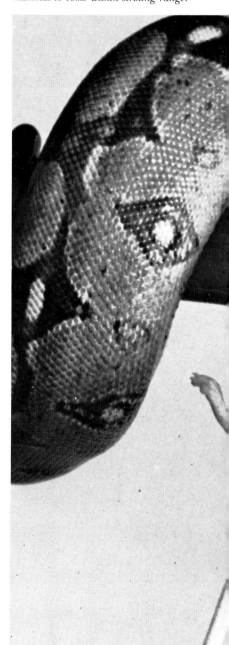

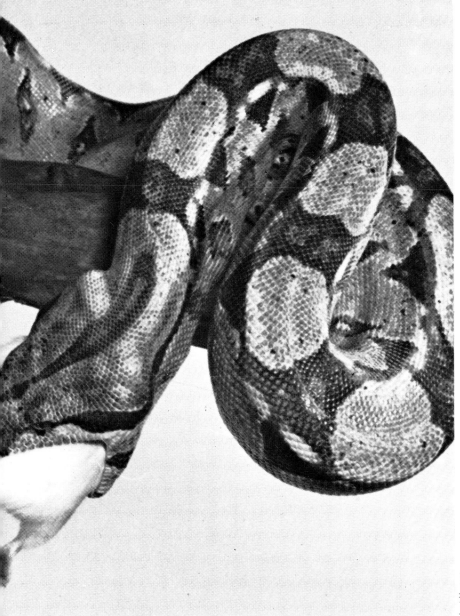

△ *Only a few boas live outside the New World and one of them is this sand boa of Africa and Asia.*
▽ *Boa constrictor engulfing a rat. The boa is often overrated as to size, but they are still big snakes, the record being 18½ ft long. Specimens over 10 ft long are rare.*

flee or to threaten by hissing, a noise like escaping steam that can be heard over a distance of 100 ft. Despite all the hair-raising stories told about boas, they prefer to live a quiet life and only as a last resort defend themselves by biting.

Clues to past history

Were it not for the boas and pythons we should have no direct evidence that the ancestors of snakes had limbs. That would have been a reasonable assumption based on their many lizard-like features but the constrictor snakes actually have the clear remains of a pelvis (or hipbone) and vestiges of hind legs. The pelvis has the same number of bones as in lizards, but they are smaller and not joined to the backbone. The limbs are represented by one, sometimes two bones and a claw, on each side of the body. There are three other kinds of snakes that show vestiges of hind limbs, or a pelvis. Blind snakes have a rod of cartilage where the pelvis should be, and thread snakes have a small pelvis and a pair of claw-shaped hind limbs. The cylinder snakes also possess rudimentary limbs and pelvis. .

There are many vestigial organs known, in both animals and ourselves. The appendix, the blind tube attached to our intestine, which was once a large sac for digesting vegetable matter is the vestigial organ that most readily springs to mind as it often leads to emergency operations. With this, as with so many others, it is wrong to say, as is often said, that it is useless. Vestigial organs have so often been found to have taken on a new function. The hind limbs of the boa offer a case in point. From being locomotory organs they have degenerated, and are now used for stimulating the female to mate.

class	**Reptilia**
order	**Squamata**
suborder	**Serpentes**
family	**Boidae**
genus & species	*Boa constrictor*

Unlike the related anaconda, the boa shows little preference for water. It is found from Mexican desert fringes to dense American jungles.

Boa *(Boa constrictor)*

387

When alert the boatbill, a heron-like bird, shows its short crest of black feathers.

PA White

The boatbill usually sits in a hunched position, the neck being hardly visible at all.

Zool Soc London

A boatbill chick has two egg-teeth, not one, to hack its way through the eggshell.

C Warner

Boatbill

There is only one species, in a family on its own, of this medium sized heron-like bird. It looks most like the night-herons but is peculiar in having a short, very broad flat bill which is as wide as the broad head. Its head and body are about 2 ft long, with a wing-span of about 2½ ft. It weighs about 21 oz. Its colour is silvery-grey with black on the crown and upper back, and a short crest of black feathers. The forehead, throat and breast are white, the sides of the body being black. The middle of the belly and the under tail feathers are rufous.

The large eye has a dark brown iris, with a greenish-yellow eyelid. The bill is black, the throat pouch and the feet are yellowish.

The boatbill has four pairs of powder down, not three as in true herons.

Secretive habits

The boatbill is an unusually secretive bird. It is more or less solitary, living in swamps with thick shrubbery or forests near freshwater lagoons and rivers or mangrove swamps. Nocturnal, it hides by day in thick foliage, not coming out to feed until late dusk, so it is seldom seen even by those living locally. Moreover, although it scolds loudly at night, in higher tones than the night-herons, which it resembles, it flies direct into cover at the slightest disturbance, doing so even at the first flash of torchlight. Its voice has been likened to a frog-like croaking, at other times it is a squawk or a bark. It also is said to rattle or clap its bill, as do other herons.

Although ranging over a wide area, from Mexico through Central America and South America as far south as Argentina, as well as in Trinidad, the boatbill's secretive behaviour has meant that, until recently, little more was known about it than the colours in its plumage. Then a small amount

of study in the field took place and finally live specimens began to trickle into zoos.

Scooping bill

The bill is used as a scoop, rather than a spear as in typical herons, to catch insects, crustaceans and other small invertebrates living in water.

Nest is a platform of sticks

Males and females, which look alike, pair and make a platform of sticks for a nest, in midsummer, in thick shrubbery. The eggs, two to four in number, are white, slightly spotted with brown at the large end, and measure 2 in. by 1½ in. One field worker in Mexico found, in late August, nestlings at all stages as well as nests with eggs. The period of incubation is unknown. The nestlings on hatching have a short triangular bill, with an egg-tooth on the tip of both upper and lower parts. The first downy feathers are white on the underside and grey on the upper parts, with brownish-black down on the crown. Immature birds are cinnamon-rufous on the upper parts and black on the top of the head.

Two egg-teeth unusual

Perhaps the most singular feature of this odd-man-out of the herons is that the chick should have two egg-teeth, one on the tip of each mandible. In many birds and reptiles, the young hack their way out of the shell by means of an excrescence at the tip of the upper mandible, known as the egg-tooth. This is shed soon after hatching.

A bird's egg especially is highly resistant to pressure from the outside but is readily broken from the inside. Even so, a chick at the moment of hatching is still very weak except for one muscle in the back of the neck known as the hatching muscle. This becomes particularly well-developed as the moment for hatching approaches and using it the chick directs its beak upwards and begins to hammer the shell. What follows differs from one species to another. Some

young birds chip away until there is a hole large enough to push the head through. Others make a row of small breaks from right to left, because as it hammers it is moving its body round.

Most small birds take 10–20 minutes, from the first peck until they finally struggle out of the shell. Others take much longer. The baby coot may take three days. An albatross may take as long as four days, or as short as 33 hours. The times thus vary even within a species, depending on circumstances. In dry weather eggs may lose too much moisture. Then the membranes surrounding the chick as well as the shell itself become tougher and harder to rupture. A bird incubating will, in hot weather, leave the nest to bathe. This is for her own comfort. But returning to the nest with damp feathers she keeps the inside of the nest damp, and moistens the eggs, so helping the chicks when they are ready to hatch.

class	**Aves**
order	**Ciconiiformes**
family	**Cochleariidae**
genus & species	***Cochlearius cochlearius***

Boatbill
(Cochlearius cochlearius)

Bobcat

The wildcat of America. Although there are other cats, the puma and lynx for instance, in the United States, the bobcat is much smaller and is comparable with the European wildcat. On average, bobcats weigh 15–20 lb, but a record is 39 lb. The total length of the body is around $2\frac{1}{2}$–3 ft, with the tail accounting for about 6 in. The closely related lynx is readily distinguished as its longer tail has a black tip while that of the bobcat has a black bar on the upper side fringed with white hairs.

The colour of the body varies considerably between different races and can often be linked with the habitat. In general, the colour is a shade of brown spotted with grey or white, but buff bobcats are common in desert country, whereas those from the forests are darker.

The ears are tipped with pointed tufts of hair, less prominent than those of the lynx. Experiments suggest that the tufts improve the efficiency of the ear in collecting sounds and that captive bobcats with clipped ear tufts do not respond so readily to sounds.

The name bobcat is linked with the short tail, and, probably, with a lolloping gait, reminiscent of a rabbit.

Wide ranging hunter

Bobcats are solitary animals and much of their hunting is done by night, so they are not often seen, although a good number of bobcats may be quartering the same area. Their home range varies with the abundance of food. They may roam over an area as much as 50 miles in diameter, or as little as 5 miles. A hunter in Wyoming once caught 39 bobcats in one spot over a period of 13 weeks.

The trails used by the bobcats can be traced, not only by footprints but also by scratches on tree trunks where the bobcats have stretched and sharpened their claws just like a domestic cat. They also have favourite spots for defaecating and urinating. Faeces and urine are covered by scratching a mound of earth over them.

Bobcats are found in all parts of the United States except the midwestern corn belt, throughout Mexico and in the southernmost part of Canada. Because they are small and can easily hide and feed on a variety of prey, they have survived the spread of agriculture much better than their cousin the lynx. Sometimes agriculture benefits the bobcats by providing them with a ready supply of food in the form of calves and lambs.

The bobcat is a good tree climber and will often seek refuge in a tree when hunted by a man with a pack of dogs. The trunk of this tree shows scratch marks where the bobcat has climbed up and down, a typical sign of bobcat country.

389

Fearless carnivore

Along with its retiring habits, the wide range of food taken has been cited as a reason for the continued abundance of bobcats in areas where the face of the countryside has been greatly changed. Rabbits and rodents such as deermice, wood rats and squirrels form the bulk of their diet. Birds and domestic animals are also eaten.

Other items are eaten occasionally. These include snakes, skunks, opossums, grasshoppers, bats and, very rarely, fruit. Porcupines are often attacked when there is a shortage of other food and porcupine quills have been found in bobcat's faeces, but usually the bobcat comes out second best in such an encounter. Bobcats have often been found with quills in their paws and mouths. In such cases the fight with the porcupine would probably have condemned the bobcat to die of starvation, as a mouthful of quills makes eating impossible.

Bobcats are very strong for their size and will attack and kill adult pronghorns and deer, as well as domestic livestock. The bobcat stalks its prey then throws itself onto the unsuspecting animal's back, biting at the base of its skull and tearing with its claws until the prey drops.

Mother fiercely defends kits

Kits may be born during any month of the year, but usually in late February or March. Occasionally a bobcat will have two litters a year. Gestation takes 50–60 days and the kits are blind for their first week. They are born in a den, in caves, under logs, or even under barns and sheds. There are usually two kits in a litter but three or four are not uncommon. Their mother defends them vigorously and the father is kept well away from the den, until the kits are weaned, when he helps the female collect food.

Hunted by men with dogs

Bobcats have been persecuted by man for their soft fur or merely for sport, and because the cats kill livestock and game birds. In some states bounties are given for bobcats and they are taken by traps or shooting, usually with hounds to flush them. When hunted with packs of dogs, bobcats often run in a wide circle, finally retreating up a tree near the start of the chase. They will often take to water or to swamps where they can outpace the dogs either by swimming or by bounding over shallow water.

Adult bobcats are killed by pumas and the young by foxes and horned owls.

A cat with a bad name

The term 'wildcat' has been used in conjunction with various activities, but not with the obvious meaning of ferocity. Wildcat strikes may appear to be acts of savagery to employers but it is difficult to see how the name came to be applied even with active pickets enforcing the strike. Wildcat oil-drilling is even more unlikely.

In these terms 'wildcat' is used to denote a risk or uncertain chance, where the course of events is not settled. Wildcat is applied to oil-drilling taking place in unproven oil-fields where there is no certainty of striking oil and the company can only bore holes and hope that oil will come up. The origin of this term appears to spring from the picture of a wildcat or bobcat that appeared on the notes issued by a mid-western bank during the early part of the last century. These notes were issued with virtually no financial backing and were therefore risky things to deal with. Other banks did similar business and became known as wildcat banks. Gradually the term spread to cover any unsound commercial enterprise involving a risk, and to other fields.

class	**Mammalia**
order	**Carnivora**
family	**Felidae**
genus & species	*Lynx rufus*

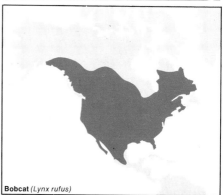

Bobcat *(Lynx rufus)*

Joe Van Wormer: Photo Res.

◁ *The bobcat probably gets its name from the short tail and its lolloping gait, which is rather like that of the rabbit. Its brown coat, spotted with grey, makes a good camouflage. Its range may extend over as much as 50 miles.*

△ *The ear tufts seem to help in sound detection, and the whiskers feel the way in the dark. This photo-portrait of a bobcat clearly shows the spot on the back of the ears which is present in all the cat family and is used in signalling.*

▽ *Bobcat on elk kill. The bobcat is very strong for its size and will even kill farm livestock. After stalking its prey it will jump onto its back, biting and clawing at the base of the skull and neck until the animal drops.*

Rod Allen: Photo Res.

Anthony Bannister: NHPA

Cotton bollworm burrowing into a tomato. It is also called corn worm and tomato fruit worm according to the plant on which it is feeding.

Bollworm

This name is applied to the caterpillars of several species of moth which attack the bolls or seed pods of cotton. The most important is the American or cotton bollworm, a very severe pest of cotton and the worst pest of maize in the United States. The caterpillar, or worm, is light green, pink or brown, with lighter underparts. The head is yellow and there are alternating light and dark stripes running down the length of the body. The adult is a moth with wings $1\frac{1}{2}$ in. from tip to tip, and variable in colour. The forewings are usually light grey-brown, while the hindwings are white with dark spots and irregular markings.

Another bad pest is the pink bollworm, that was once estimated to be the sixth most destructive insect in the world. The worms are $\frac{1}{2}$ in. long and pinkish-white on the upper surface. The adult is a small moth $\frac{3}{4}$ in. from wingtip to wingtip. It flies by night and looks like a clothes moth with narrow, pointed wings.

The Egyptian bollworm is the caterpillar of another small moth which flourishes in hot, dry conditions and is common in the southern part of Egypt.

Widespread range

The cotton bollworm is widespread throughout the tropical and warm temperate regions of the world. It is occasionally found in Britain, where the moth is called the scarce bordered straw, and regarded as a great prize by collectors if found in the wild. Adults are blown in from the Continent and

caterpillars are imported in tomatoes and other fresh vegetables, but they are never able to survive the winter, so have not become established in Britain.

The pink bollworm is thought to have been a native of India but it spread rapidly to other cotton-growing countries in Asia, and to the Philippines and Hawaii. It has also been introduced to Africa, Australia, Brazil, Egypt, West Indies and Mexico.

Not just a cotton feeder

The cotton bollworm is by no means limited to feeding on cotton or maize (known as corn in the United States). It is also a pest of tobacco, tomatoes, beans, vetch, melons, oranges and many other plants. Because of this it is given a number of names depending on the crop it is attacking. The most usual names are cotton bollworm, corn worm and tomato fruit worm. The moths feed on the nectar of many kinds of flowers, usually at dusk, but they can be seen about on warm, cloudy days.

Life cycle of destruction

The eggs of the cotton bollworm are laid singly on the leaves and petals of the food plant, and one moth will lay 500–3 000. Each one is hemispherical and ridged, resembling a minute sea urchin, half the size of a pinhead. The eggs hatch in 10 days and the caterpillars start eating the leaves, petals and developing fruit. The damage they can cause is increased because a caterpillar does not stay in one cotton boll or tomato. It will eat its way in, then turn and bore another way out, and crawl over to another fruit and repeat the process. In this way a single caterpillar can destroy all the fruits on one branch.

The damage to the crops is caused in several ways. Leaves and petals may wither

and fall. Early in the season the blossoms may fail to open, and if the attack comes later, the fruits are made worthless, since the seeds are eaten and the fleecy cotton or lint fails to develop or becomes stunted. Where the fruits are sold for eating, the presence or mere signs of worm infestation prevent them from being sold. This is a serious problem for corn-growers, for in the worst years over 90% of the ears in a crop may be attacked and so made worthless.

When the caterpillars are full-grown, they crawl down the stem, or just let go and drop to the ground, then burrow into the ground to a depth of 2–6 in. and pupate in smooth-walled cells. The adult moth emerges from the pupa 10–25 days later, depending on the climate, and crawls back up the tunnel that was eaten out by the caterpillar.

There are three or four generations each year. The first two pass their lives on maize, tobacco and other plants. Cotton is attacked by the third generation, in August or later. The pupae of the final generation pass the winter in the soil and the adults emerge the next spring.

Pest control problem

It is almost impossible to expect the total eradication of an insect pest, but what farmers can aim for is the reduction of the pests' numbers to such a degree that they have little effect on the crops, or they can take measures to prevent the pests spreading. The latter is more difficult now that transport is so rapid and goods are regularly shipped around the world. This is shown by the spread of the pink bollworm. It was imported to Mexico in cotton from Egypt in 1911. In 1917 it was found in Texas. The difficulty with this bollworm is that the caterpillar spends the winter in a cocoon

△ *Aerial insecticide attack on bollworm.*

▽ *Bollworms eat seeds of cotton boll so the fleecy cotton fails to grow or becomes stunted.*

in the stored seed, or in the ground, and it can remain like this for over 2 years. Luckily, it is quite easy to control its spread by heating the seed for a short time at 55°C/131°F. This kills the caterpillar but not the seed. The caterpillars in the ground can be killed by leaving a fallow period in which no cotton is grown on infected soil.

Populations of bollworms can be kept down by deep ploughing in the winter which allows predators such as birds and rodents, as well as the weather, to destroy the resting caterpillars and pupae. The cotton bollworm's depredations can also be reduced by early planting of cotton so that the third generation of caterpillars does not have so much time to cause damage. Since the Second World War, DDT and other chemical insecticides have been used against bollworms, but once they have eaten into the bolls they are safe from the chemicals. Now, experiments are being made to find biological controlling agents, that is, predatory animals that will keep the numbers of the pests down. Spiders seem to be suitable for this as they will follow the caterpillars right into the bolls. Observations are being made as to which spiders are most suitable. It is important to find ones which feed readily on bollworms and are active when bollworms are attacking crops.

class	**Insecta**
order	**Lepidoptera**
family	**Noctuidae**
genera & species	***Heliothis armigera*** *cotton bollworm* ***Earias insulana*** *Egyptian bollworm*
family	**Gelechiidae**
genus & species	***Pectinophora gossypiella*** *pink bollworm, others*

Frail foodfish

As it is so easily disfigured in the confusion of trawl nets, the Bombay duck is seldom seen undamaged. Little is known of its life and habits, but the streamlined shape and wide, gaping jaws suggest it may be a fast, voracious feeder, and the conspicuous barbed teeth are characteristic of deep-sea fishes.

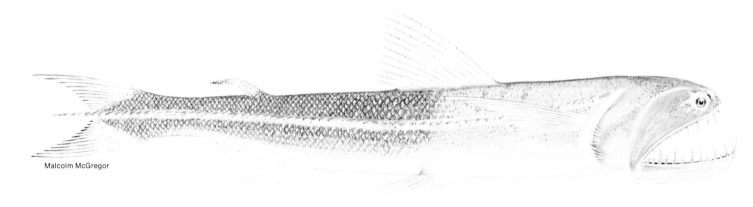

Malcolm McGregor

Bombay duck

Not a bird but a fish! When dried and salted it is an almost indispensable addition to an Indian curry. It was originally called the bummelo or bummalo by Europeans in 1673 (sometimes spelt bummelow) but was later given the name by which it is now better known. This is an alteration of the Indian name bombil by assimilation to the place name, Bombay. 'Duck' is a fanciful addition.

Bombay duck is an elongate, compressed, salmon-type fish with a maximum length of 16 in., although most of those caught are well below this. It has a stout head and short snout. The mouth is wide and the teeth are barbed at the tips, those of the lower jaw being longer than those in the upper jaw. The body is covered with thin transparent scales. The paired fins are long, each pelvic fin having 9 rays. The dorsal fin is relatively large, there is a small fleshy fin, and the tail fin has a third, small lobe.

From Zanzibar to China

The Bombay duck occurs suddenly and mysteriously in large numbers at certain times of the year in the surface waters of parts of the Indian Ocean and its total range has been stated to be from Zanzibar to China.

This fish appears in large numbers off Bombay during June to September and occurs elsewhere in other months. Although a marine fish it readily enters estuaries where the water is brackish and at times ascends far up rivers.

It is commonly said that the body of Bombay duck glows with a brilliantly phosphorescent light when freshly caught, due to bacteria in the surface slime, but Dr Stanley Kemp looked into this in 1917 and was unable to corroborate the story.

Feeding

There is little information, apart from the results of examining a few stomachs, about the food of Bombay duck. These suggest that it eats shrimps and small fishes, possibly also small cuttlefishes. It is said to be a voracious feeder.

Enemies

Sharks and large predatory fishes are said sometimes to feed on shoals of Bombay duck.

Life history unknown

Little information is available. Individuals taken far out to sea in February and March contained ripe eggs and active spermatozoa.

Mystery fish

Although Bombay duck has long been a favourite relish, well-known to British residents in India and to those dining in Indian restaurants in this country, our knowledge of it as a living fish is scanty and in some respects contradictory. It appears in large numbers in the monsoon periods off the coasts of India. Sunder Lal Hora, who made a lifelong study of the fishes of India, has suggested that they come inshore at those times because there is a large volume of well-oxygenated water entering the sea from the great rivers swollen by the monsoon rains. He also suggests that this freshwater carries large quantities of nutrient salts washed down from the soil on the mountains and plains of India. This acts as a fertiliser for the millions of minute plants of the plankton floating, and growing in the sunshine, near the surface of the sea. The animals of the plankton, including various species of shrimps, feed on the plant plankton and so there is a sudden increase in the fish's food supply. This may be an added attraction to the Bombay duck.

What happens during the rest of the year is still unsolved. The Bombay duck seems to be an oceanic species, coming inshore for the rich feed and then migrating back. The fish itself is of delicate build, easily damaged in the trawl, in the way delicate deep-sea fishes are damaged. The outward appearance of the fish alone, especially its large mouth and conspicuous barbed teeth, suggests a deep-sea fish.

Luminous wanderer

The evidence of its luminosity is conflicting. There is the general assertion, which is still being made in authoritative books, that the slime on the body is phosphorescent. This would not necessarily indicate a deep-sea species because this is a character of some fishes that live in surface waters. More recent authors say that the fish carries definite light organs, typical of deep-sea fishes.

The best that can be said, at the moment, is that the Bombay duck is a wanderer. But whether its wanderings constitute a migration or are simply nomadism has yet to be seen.

class	**Osteichthyes**
order	**Salmoniformes**
family	**Harpodontidae**
genus & species	***Harpodon nehereus***

Bonito hunt in shoals, using smell and sight to detect their prey and change colour with 'excitement' at making a kill.

DH Prescott: Marineland Pacific

Bonito

This name is applied to several species of the mackerel family. The one chosen here as a representative, Sarda sarda, *might almost be called the common bonito. It is found on both sides of the Atlantic, mainly in tropical or subtropical waters but occurring sparingly in temperate waters. It is up to 2 ft long, shaped like a tunny, with a streamlined body and a series of finlets behind the dorsal and anal fins. The colour is steel-blue and there are dark stripes on the upper part of the body.*

The name bonito (also spelt boneta or bonita) is of Spanish origin, first coming into use in 1599. There is a related species in the central and western Pacific and a third in the eastern Pacific, from California to Chile. Most of our knowledge comes from this one, S. chilensis, *studied in the California seaquarium. Species belonging to other genera, also in the mackerel family, are known as stripe-bellied bonito and plain bonito.*

All bonito are caught commercially or for game and their white meat is canned.

Hunting fish

Bonito are hunting fish which swim in shoals when young, becoming more solitary with increasing age. Small bonito often shelter in groups under floating timber and big ones used to follow sailing ships, pursuing flying fishes flushed by the vessels.

Bonito have no gas filled swimbladder to give them buoyancy and are heavier than seawater, but they can keep at a constant depth by cruising at 2 mph with the pectoral fins spread to give the body lift by their planing action in the water. The fish swims with closed mouth which is opened at intervals to allow water to pass across the gills. The highest speed recorded was 10 mph, about half that of tunny. They travel about 42 miles in 24 hours.

Colourful feeding

Bonito hunt by sight but their feeding behaviour is also stimulated by fluids liberated into the water from the bodies of their prey. Bonito make a quick dash at a small fish and at the same time there is a change in the colour pattern of the bonito. Vertical dark bars appear on the flanks, superimposed on the normal oblique stripes, and a yellow stripe appears along the midline of the back. When a bonito is caught on a hook and lifted from the water this is the pattern it has, the result of swimming at the bait or lure. The colour pattern returns to normal when the fish is full and then the sight of food evokes no feeding behaviour. The natural prey is small fishes and, like mackerel, bonito are caught by trolling with a lure and a hidden hook. Progress of the bonito when feeding is marked by a thrashing of the surface and by watchful attendant birds overhead. Small fish are caught head-first or, if held crosswise in the mouth, there is a quick sideways movement of the bonito's head and the fish is shifted to a headfirst position and then swallowed.

Young bonito are preyed upon by predatory fishes, including adult bonitos, which themselves may be taken by tunny.

Seaquarium studies reveal courtship

It is always assumed that in fishes that spawn in shoals, there is no courtship behaviour, that the ova and sperm are liberated into the sea and that fertilisation of the ova is at random. The studies in the Californian seaquarium revealed a definite courtship.

The female swims along a wobbling course with the male swimming close behind her in a normal way, or he may swim in tight circles. The male may swim so close behind her under these circumstances that his nose is touching her tailfins. The wobbling action will occur when a sexually excited male swims towards a female, or a female may start swimming in this way, as if to attract the male. Another circumstance showing this behaviour is connected with pair-formation. If another male comes near, the courting male will swim away from the female and range himself alongside the second male. There is no physical contact but both show the vertical dark bars and the yellow line along the back.

Coldblooded flirts

Perhaps the one exciting result from the studies of bonito in the seaquarium is this reorientation of knowledge. It has always been tacitly assumed that fishes spawning in shoals merely cast their reproductive cells, their eggs or milt, into the water where fertilisation occurs entirely at random. To put it in more ordinary language, we have always looked on shoal spawning as a cold-blooded, unromantic affair. Now we see that in at least one species, and probably in all shoaling fishes, the individuals pair up to spawn. Moreover, in their simple way the bonito shoals seem to have the same jealousies, rivalries between males, even the female flirts, found in any other species.

class	**Osteichthyes**
order	**Perciformes**
family	**Scombridae**
genus & species	*Sarda sarda, others*

John Visser

Bontebok

A species of antelope very closely related to the blesbok (see p. 376). Some writers consider them to be races of the same species. However, although they interbreed in captivity the offspring have not yet been shown to be fertile, so the bontebok and blesbok belong no more to the same species than do the horse and the ass which produce the sterile mule.

Bontebok are a little larger than blesbok, standing over 4 ft at the shoulder and weighing up to 200 lb. They have the same glossy hair on the rump that has been described as being like the 'bloom' on a plum but the bontebok does not have the brown line between the eyes that divides the white blaze on the face of a blesbok, and it has a very conspicuous white rump. The horns grow to 15 or 16 in.

Saved from extinction

The bontebok was well known to the early Dutch settlers in South Africa as it lives in the lower coastal area of the Cape Province, the region first colonized south of the Orange River. They did not discover the very similar blesbok which lives on higher ground, on the plains of the Karroo and the high veldt of the Transvaal, until they trekked north in the 19th century. The name bontebok means pied or painted buck, after the white blaze, white rump and white on the insides of the legs.

Unfortunately, being so accessible, the bontebok suffered from the hunters far more than the more remote, inland, blesbok. They would have been exterminated early in the last century if it had not been for the efforts of a few farmers. Even then a licence from a magistrate was needed to kill bontebok and a heavy fine was imposed on poachers. This only slowed down the process of extermination, however, for

some smallholders deliberately planted corn to entice the animals onto their land so they could shoot them at night. The extermination was only halted by a Mr Alexander Van der Byl of Bredasdorp who, when enclosing his farm, thought of driving the bontebok from the neighbouring plain into the enclosure. About 30, a large proportion of the remaining population, were captured in this way, and apart from a few wild herds, bontebok soon existed only on his farm and those of some of his neighbours who followed suit.

Breeding

The calves are dropped from September to October. When they are a week old they can outrun a horseman.

Fast runner to escape enemies

As with blesbok, lions and leopards were their chief enemies, but now they are little molested. Not only are the carnivores,

Jean Dorste WWF

The painted buck

Far left: Bontebok on Cape Point Nature Reserve, South Africa. Bontebok were nearly wiped out by hunters early in the last century but were saved when a farmer enclosed some on his land and established a breeding herd.

Left: The bontebok can be distinguished from the very similar blesbok by the white blaze on the face not being divided between the eyes and the relatively conspicuous white patch on the rump.

Overleaf: The home of bontebok is the coastal area of Cape Province in S Africa. They are therefore separated from the blesbok which live on higher ground, so although they eat the same food they do not compete and have evolved separately.

especially the leopard, becoming rare, but the few bontebok are now kept in enclosures, such as the Cape Point nature reserve, where they are usually safe.

When alarmed bontebok run against the wind. They are very fast and are capable of great endurance. When pressed they run with their heads down and noses almost touching the grass.

Double-dutch names

The bontebok was the common small antelope familiar to the Dutch Boer settlers around the Cape of Good Hope. They had known it for 100 years when some of them started to move inland to find new areas in which to settle, preferably away from the interfering British. As they moved up on to the open plains which were more suitable for cultivation than the lower wooded areas more antelopes were seen. They were very little different from the antelopes around

the Cape and were, accordingly, also called bontebok. In fact, some plains to the south of the Orange River are still known as 'bontebok-flats'. In 1836 the Boers crossed the Orange River and many more of the antelopes were seen. The old settlers who had been born and bred in the country continued to call them bontebok but the new settlers called them blesbok after the white blaze on the face.

This, of course, has led to confusion and is a good instance of the need for unambiguous Latin names for species. Unfortunately, there is even confusion in the Latin names because some zoologists decided the two antelopes were so similar that they were really one species, with the differences in size and colour only separating them into races. This is now generally accepted.

Their ability to produce offspring, although sterile, shows that they must, indeed, be very closely related and they probably descended from a not-too-distant

ancestor but became separated – the one on lowland, the other on highland plains. In isolation they have evolved separately to form two species.

Here we see an example of the zoological principle, elaborated under booby (see p 400), whereby two closely related species cannot live in the same place and eat the same food. The various species of boobies live in the same place but live on different food, whereas the bontebok and blesbok eat the same food, grass, but do not compete against each other as they live in different places.

class	**Mammalia**
order	**Artiodactyla**
family	**Bovidae**
genus & species	***Damaliscus dorcas dorcas***

Booby

Booby is a name applied to six species of the gannet family that are confined to the tropical regions. It is derived from the Spanish 'bobo' meaning dunce. This is an allusion to their clumsiness on land and their lack of fear of man.

Boobies are goose-sized birds, heavily built with thick necks and large heads. The bill is stout, broad at the base and tapering to a point. The wings are long and pointed and boobies are powerful and agile fliers, their flight contrasting

of the widespread boobies is the white, masked or blue-faced booby. Its plumage is, again, mainly white with blue-black naked skin on the face and yellow to greenish-blue feet.

The other three boobies are confined to certain ranges. The Peruvian booby or 'Piquero' is one of the guano-producing birds and is the commonest bird of the cool Humboldt current that runs up the coast of Chile and Peru. The blue-footed booby, with its distinctive mottled brown and white body and bright blue feet, also lives on the west coast of America but is confined to the warmer waters from

the boobies dive from the surface of the sea.

The Peruvian boobies feed largely on anchovies (see p. 127) but flying fish are a popular food throughout the boobies' range. These are not caught while airborne but are taken just after they have plunged back into the sea after a flight. Boobies will often follow ships, preying on the flying fish scared out of the water by the bow waves.

Careless colonial breeders

Breeding takes place at different times, depending on climate, sea conditions and species. At Ascension Island in the middle of the Atlantic Ocean where boobies have been studied in detail, the white booby breeds all the year round but the peak of

FGH Allen

Brown booby demonstrating its powerful wings and aerobatic ability.

René E Honegger WWF

Blue-footed booby descending onto its nest.

with their clumsiness on land in the same way as albatrosses (see p. 64).

Three species of booby are widespread in tropical regions, breeding on coasts and islands and feeding over the sea. Their common names describe their distinguishing features. The brown booby, which is the commonest in many parts of the tropics, differs from the others in not having an almost wholly white body. Its upper parts are dark brown, while the underparts are white. Around the bill and under the throat there is a patch of bare skin which is dark blue in males and yellow in females.

The red-footed booby is mainly white with black primary wing feathers and a grey-brown tail. On the ground it can be seen to have red feet. The bare skin on the head is black and red. The third

California to Peru. Abbott's booby is found in the Indian Ocean. It breeds on Assumption Island and Christmas Island, where it nests in trees.

Aerobatics and underwater swimming

Soaring perhaps 100 ft above the sea, the boobies can be seen partly to close their wings and plummet down, crashing, bill first, into the water. The shock of the impact is cushioned by air sacs under the skin of the head and damage to the brain is prevented by a specially strong skull. This spectacular display is a method used by all of the gannet family to catch the fish and squid on which they feed. Fish are chased by swimming with both wings and feet, for rather than catching the fish by spearing it as they dive the boobies catch them from underneath as they return to the surface. The spectacular high-diving is not always used; sometimes

egglaying is June and July with only a few clutches started during November, December and January. On the other hand, the egglaying of the brown booby is more spaced out and there are peaks of laying in April and December.

All boobies nest in colonies with the birds usually crowded together but nesting sites vary. White boobies nest on the flat tops of cliffs while the brown boobies choose more inaccessible places along the ledges on the cliff faces. Red-footed boobies and Abbott's boobies nest in trees or bushes and are remarkably agile in this arboreal life.

Pairs are slow to form and there is a prolonged courtship, but once formed the pair stay together for life. Like the albatrosses (see p. 64) the boobies have an elaborate courtship dance. The male cocks his tail up and goose-steps, lifting his feet as high as possible and puffing out his breast. Sometimes he merely marks time, paddling in one place, then he struts up and down and eventually turns towards the female and, raising his wings, he emits a whistle. This is repeated several times, then the strutting continues. At first the female takes little notice of this performance but later she becomes more demonstrative, leaning forward to touch the male's bill or neck.

The nest is built of guano (the dried droppings of the birds themselves), seaweed, feathers or fish bones which the male collects and deposits in front of the female as she builds up a cup-shaped nest. Two eggs are laid but rarely is more than one chick reared. Eggs are sometimes kicked out of the nest as the incubating bird flies off. However, any eggs that a sitting booby can reach with its bill it will roll back into the nest, with the result that boobies are sometimes found sitting on six or seven eggs that have been retrieved after being knocked out of their neighbours' nests.

Boobies do not have a brood patch, the area of bare skin on the breast where the eggs are kept warm. Instead the webs of their feet develop a rich network of blood vessels which supply heat to the eggs balanced on their feet.

Both parents incubate the eggs, taking turns of a few hours each. When not incubating or feeding the boobies congregate with immature birds in groups called clubs outside the breeding colony.

Eggs hatch after 6 or 7 weeks and the chicks emerge naked and helpless. After a fortnight they are covered in a white down and in 5 months they have grown a full covering of feathers and are ready to take to the air. Unlike gannets, young boobies are fed by their parents after they have left the nest, sometimes for as long as four months.

Enemies steal food

Frigate birds and kelp gulls, a species of South American gull almost identical with the lesser black-backed gull, frequently nest near booby colonies and prey upon them. The frigate birds steal the boobies' food by chasing them, grabbing their tails and flipping them over. This panics the boobies into disgorging their food which the frigate birds catch. Kelp gulls raid the booby colonies for eggs and chicks. Sometimes a pair will work together, one attracting the attention of a sitting booby, drawing it off its nest, while the other sneaks up behind

White booby defending its chick. Clumsy on land, its webbed feet make it an efficient swimmer.

John Warham

and steals an egg. Peruvian boobies were once wantonly exploited by man for their guano.

Relatives do not compete

It is a principle of zoology that if two related species of animal are living in the same place they will eat different kinds of food, or if they eat the same kind of food they will live in different places. In this way they avoid competing with each other for the available food supplies. Where it does happen that there is an overlap, in food and habitat, one species will become dominant, the other being much less abundant.

The difference in diet or habitat need not be very distinct. One species may feed during the day, the other at night, or one may feed on the tops of trees, the other on the bottom branches. Studies on the brown and white boobies, both of which nest on Ascension Island, showed that these two closely related birds, nesting in the same area, avoided direct competition for food. In the first place, the proportions of the different kinds of fish in their diets varied. The brown booby dives less steeply than the white booby, penetrating less far into the water, and so it feeds on the surface-living fish. Furthermore, the brown booby takes shorter spells on the nest than the white booby. Therefore when it goes out fishing it has less time, so its feeding grounds are closer inshore than those of the white booby.

This alone effectively prevents the two species from drawing upon the same food supplies, but the differences in breeding season also means that their peak require-ments for food do not coincide. Most brown boobies lay eggs in April and December, while white boobies have a peak egg-laying time in June and July, so the times when they need to catch large quantities of food for their chicks are well apart.

This principle shows us that we must think not just about the way animals are made but about the way they live and reproduce, what they eat and what eats them, to understand them fully.

class	**Aves**
order	**Pelecaniformes**
family	**Sulidae**
genus & species	*Sula sula* red-footed booby *S. leucogaster* brown booby *S. dactylatra* white booby *S. nebouxii* blue-footed booby *S. variegata* Peruvian booby *S. abbotti* Abbott's booby

Pair of blue-footed boobies with their down-covered young. These birds are confined to the warmer waters of the west coast of America from California to Peru.

Close up of a booby's head showing the naked skin on the face.

White booby on South Meyer Island, New Zealand. These birds are widespread, the one on page 265 is on Raine Island, Australia, those below right on Galapagos and above right on Seychelles.

White, masked, or blue-faced booby on Hood Island, Galapagos, looking at the photographer.

Peterson; Photo Res.

John Tashjian at San Diego Zoo

CR Veitch NZ Wildlife Service

ES Hobson

A nesting colony of white boobies on Desnoeufs Island, Seychelles, sharing their home with sooty terns *Sterna fuscata* *(the smaller black and white birds in the background)* and, probably, in the air, brown noddies *Anous stolidus and frigate birds* Fregata aquila.

This young down-covered white booby, with its parent, takes 5 months to grow its flight feathers.

KB Newman

Boomslang —
tree-top terror

The boomslang's venom is very strong and its agility both in trees and on the ground make it a most effective killer. Fortunately, although more poisonous than both mambas and cobras, it secretes only a very small amount of venom; also it is very shy, so it will rarely strike and prove fatal to man.

Okapia

John Visser

It is one of the rear fanged snakes in which some of the back teeth in the upper jaw carry the venom. A boomslang's victim dies a slow death as it is seized in the jaws and held firmly while the venom trickles down the grooves in the teeth and acts on the victim.

▷ *These boomslangs' prehensile tails help them to hang motionless with the front parts of their bodies raised in the air. This trick has been known to deceive birds into perching on such a fatal 'branch'.*

David Hughes

△ *If threatened a boomslang inflates its neck to show the brilliantly coloured skin between the scales, giving a frightening effect.*
◁ *Boomslangs often hide, immobile among foliage.*
▷ *They may also come down to the ground in search of food or a place to lay eggs. The female is dark brown and may be mistaken for a mamba which also moves very quickly on the ground.*
▽▷ *A distinguishing feature of the boomslang is the round blunt head and large eyes with a round pupil.*

Boomslang

The boomslang is one of the rear-fanged snakes in which some of the teeth in the back part of the upper jaw are enlarged and have grooves running down their front surfaces to carry venom. In general, rear-fanged snakes are not dangerous to man, but the boomslang is an exception.

Boomslang is the Afrikaans word for tree snake but is applied to only one of many tree-dwelling snakes. Boomslangs grow up to 6 ft in length but average around 4 ft. The body is slender, the tail long and a distinguishing feature is the round, blunt head and large eyes with round or occasionally slit-like pupil. The coloration of the body is bright green, sometimes with black patches. Females are almost always a uniform light or dark brown. The variation in colour often causes boomslangs to be confused with other species, especially mambas.

Fatal perch

The boomslang is a very agile snake amongst the trees, where it slides gracefully through the branches, aided by a prehensile tail. It often comes down to the ground, however, in search of food or a place to lay its eggs, where it can travel very rapidly, flashing back to cover if disturbed.

Much of its time is spent immobile, coiled on a branch or poised with the front part of the body raised in the air. When immobile it is very difficult to see, its green or green and black body merging with the foliage. Birds, which figure largely in its diet, have been known to perch on it.

Prey held while venom kills

The prey of boomslangs is chameleons and other tree lizards and snakes, together with birds, small mammals and frogs. An animal is seized in the jaws and held firmly while the venom trickles down the grooves in the teeth and acts on the victim. In the case of the larger reptiles it catches, this takes about 15 minutes. This is quite a slow death but the venom is very toxic, only minute quantities being needed to ensure eventual death. A pigeon succumbs after injection with only 0·0002 mg (less than one ten-thousandth of an ounce) of boomslang venom.

The eggs and fledglings of birds are often snatched from their nests and a boomslang may be mobbed by furious, yet still cautious, parent birds if they find it near their nest. Eggs are swallowed whole and the shells dissolved by the strong digestive juices.

Breeding in trees

Unlike most other snakes, which mate on the ground, boomslangs mate in trees. The eggs, 8–23 in number, are laid in early summer, 4 months after mating. The female seeks out a hollow in which to lay her eggs, perhaps a woodpecker hole in a tree or a hollow in a sandy bank, wherever it is warm and moist. The eggs hatch out after 4–7 months and the newly-emerged young measure about 15 in.

Enemies

Usually boomslangs retreat from danger but if threatened or provoked they will inflate the neck and front part of the body with air, so that they look like a cobra with its hood inflated. The distension of the body in this manner separates the scales and shows the brilliantly coloured skin between them, giving a frightening effect. Their natural enemies are therefore few. Boomslangs are, however, cannibalistic, and one can eat another nearly its own size.

Potent poison

Several snakes have been credited with being the most dangerous to man, notably the mamba, the cobra and the krait, but it is very difficult to find an outright winner because so many factors are involved. A snake with a very potent poison may not really be dangerous because it lives in inaccessible places, whereas another with mild venom may habitually haunt dwellings where it is a constant hazard. Sea snakes in Asia cause many deaths among fishermen who walk barefoot through their catch which may harbour a snake.

The boomslang is very hard to place in a hierarchy of dangerous snakes. Its pure venom is very toxic, acting both on the nervous system and on the blood system, dissolving the walls of blood vessels and destroying blood cells. The venom is more toxic, weight for weight, than that of mambas and cobras, yet each boomslang secretes only a very small amount. Added to this, boomslangs are shy and only bite if handled.

They also take some time to inject the venom, having to chew at the wound to allow the venom to penetrate. So if the snake is knocked away immediately, the bite may not be very severe. Donald Broadley, a Rhodesian herpetologist (a snake specialist), records how he was bitten on the finger by a boomslang while demonstrating snakes in the Salisbury Snake Park. He immediately pulled it off and cut incisions around the bite and encouraged a flow of blood. An hour later he developed a splitting headache and was taken to hospital. The next day blood transfusions were started to replace the destroyed blood cells and the bleeding from gums and stomach. Later blood appeared in the urine and it was only after 16 pints of blood had been transfused in the following week that the bleeding stopped. During this time he had felt no pain, only a weakness from loss of blood.

Another herpetologist was luckier. He was bitten through his shirt and very little venom entered his body. However, he was very ill for a few days. Both these men knew what to do in the event of snakebite and had access to antidotes and medical aid, but where there is neither knowledge nor medication, boomslang bites can prove fatal.

class	**Reptilia**
order	**Squamata**
sub-order	**Serpentes**
family	**Colubridae**
genus & species	*Dispholidus typus*

Few birds or tree-climbing lizards are safe from the deadly poisonous boomslang which is very agile amongst the trees and can glide gracefully to the tips of the most slender branches.

A magnificent Borzoi. Its unusual arched back and long, narrow head are characteristics of this breed.

BORZOIS

This graceful and aristocratic hound has a history going back at least three centuries. Known originally as the Russian Wolfhound, it was evolved in Russia for the specific purpose of the great sport of those days, wolf hunting.

In order to get a breed of dog that had great speed and courage Russia imported a breed known as the Arabian Greyhound, which was somewhat similar to the Saluki. Although very fast, these dogs were unfortunately not hardy enough to survive the severe Russian winters, and they all eventually perished. Russia then imported more Greyhounds and finally crossed these with a long-legged breed of the collie type from the Steppes. This introduced a thicker, wavy coat, and so was evolved the Russian Wolfhound, later to be known as the Borzoi, which means the 'swift one'. These dogs were much favoured in the days of Imperial Russia, and formed a part of the Russian aristocrat's way of life. In those days of extravagant and colourful ways of living, big hunting parties—some carrying on for weeks—were the favourite pastime of the nobility of that country. These magnificent hounds, perfectly matched in size, speed, colour and markings were usually hunted in pairs. Although today all colours are acceptable, most Borzois then were white with gold markings.

Great courage was needed as well as speed, as they were expected to bring down fully grown wolves. Killing the wolves was not expected of them–their job was to attack and hold the wolf until the huntsmen arrived to despatch it with a dagger. The strains of these dogs were jealously guarded for many years.

In 1842 Queen Victoria was presented with a pair of Borzois by the Czar of Russia. They were so favourably received that more were sent, and so the Borzoi had arrived in England. In time they became popular and were 'adopted' by the English nobility. Soon after their arrival in England the USA became interested in the breed, and Borzois were imported, firstly from England and some years later directly from Russia to win the American hearts as well.

With their size and style, they remain today one of the most lovely and spectacular hounds seen in American and European show rings. They are one of the largest hounds, for the American bred Borzoi male is up to 31 inches in height with the female at about 29 inches. They are usually slightly smaller in England.

The Russian aristocrat

When thinking of the Borzoi these five words sum it up: size, speed, symmetry, strength and style. They still need to look as though they could hunt in order to remain true to their type, therefore they have powerful loins and well-developed muscles. Their hocks are low with slightly bent stifles and strong pasterns. The back is very arched and rather bony. The coat is long and silky and can be flat, wavy or curly. The head is very unusual, being Roman nosed in profile and long and lean with a flat, narrow skull. The ears are small and thin and placed far back on the head. Its combination of great height, noticeably arched back and Roman nosed head, together with its beautiful coat make the Borzoi instantly recognisable, indeed, unmistakable. This magnificent animal has an air of great distinction and elegance.

Superb house pets

Far removed indeed from the days of wolf hunting and running at speed on the Russian plains and forests, they still need a great deal of space to run in. They are special dogs and are rather expensive to feed, as their weight can be from 75 to 105 lbs.

It seems incredible to think that in spite of being originally bred for such a savage sport as wolf hunting, Borzois make superb house pets if owned by people who appreciate them. Lovely to look at and so decorative, they remain very proud, and retain their wonderful arrogance. They adore their owners, giving great affection and responding to the love they certainly expect to receive in return. Although Borzois are gentle and kind in nature they do prefer not to have small children around them, and will tolerate them if necessary, rather than seek their company.

Bottlenose dolphin

This, known to Americans as the common porpoise, is the animal that in the last 20 years has become a star performer in the seaquaria of the United States. It is up to 12 ft long, weighs as much as 440 lb and is black above and white underneath, with a bulbous head and a marked snout. The forehead of the male is more protruding than that of the female. The moderate-sized flippers taper to a point and the fin in the middle of the back has a sharply-pointed apex directed backwards, making the hinder margin concave. It has 20—22 conical teeth in each half of both upper and lower jaw. Although as well suited to life in the water as any fish it is in fact a mammal like whales or, for that matter, man, giving birth to fully-developed young which are suckled on milk. The bottlenose is the commonest cetacean (group name of the whales) off the Atlantic coast of North America, from Florida to Maine. It occurs in the Bay of Biscay and Mediterranean also. It occasionally ranges to Britain, and is also found off West Africa, south to Dakar.

Cooperative schools

Bottlenose dolphins live in schools containing individuals of both sexes and all ages. Apparently there is no leader, but males in the school observe a 'peck order' based on size. When food is plentiful the schools may be large, breaking into smaller schools when it is scarce. The dolphins pack together at times of danger. They also assist an injured member of the school by one ranging either side of it and, pushing their heads under its flippers, raising it to the surface to breathe. In schools they keep in touch by sounds.

They sleep by night and are active by day, although each feeding session is followed by an hour's doze. Females sleep at the surface with only the blowhole exposed and this periodically opens and closes, as it does in stranded dolphins, by reflex action. The males sleep a foot below the surface, periodically rising to breathe.

The main swimming action is in the tail, with its horizontal flukes. This, the flexible part of the animal, is used with an up-and-down movement in swimming, quite unlike that of fishes, with only an occasional sideways movement. The flippers help in steering and balance. The dorsal fin also aids stability, but it is the lungs placed high up in the body that are chiefly responsible for keeping a dolphin balanced.

The depths to which bottle-nosed dolphins can dive has to be deduced from the remains of fishes in their stomachs. These show they go down for food to at least 70 ft, and they can stay submerged for up to 15 minutes. Their lung capacity is half as much again as that of a land animal and in addition they fill their lungs to capacity. Land animals, including ourselves, use only about half the lung capacity and change only 10—15% of the air in the lungs with each breath. A dolphin changes up to 90%.

Tame dolphin leaping some 30 ft into the air to take fish accurately, which proves that its small eyes are still quite useful out of water.

Popperfoto

Well equipped for marine life

Since a dolphin's lungs are compressed when diving, air would be squeezed into the bronchial tubes, where no gaseous exchange would take place, unless this were prevented by valves. There are 25—40 of these in the bronchial tubes of the bottlenose dolphin and they act as a series of taps controlling the pressure in the lungs according to whether the animal is diving, swimming on the level or rising to the surface.

At the surface the pulse of the bottlenose dolphin is 110 a minute. When submerged it drops to 50 a minute and starts to increase as the animal nears the surface. The drop is related to the way the blood circulation is shut off so that the oxygen supply goes mainly to essential organs, notably the heart and brain. This extends the time of submergence by reducing the frequency with which visits need be made to the surface to breathe.

Whales and dolphins have an insulating layer of blubber, but they have no sweat glands and they cannot pant, so other means are needed to lose excess body heat. The tail flukes and the flippers are always warmer to the touch than the rest of the body and their temperature is not only higher than that of other parts of the body but varies through a greater range. They also have a much thinner layer of blubber. It is assumed therefore that these parts lose heat to the surrounding water. In brief, whales and dolphins keep cool through their flukes and flippers.

A dolphin's eyesight is not particularly good. Yet the animal can move its eyelids, shut its eyes, even wink. At one time it was thought the eyes were of little value and were quite useless out of water. This last seems proved wrong by the way dolphins in seaquaria will leap out of water and accurately snatch fish from the attendant's hand. Moreover, the visual fields of left and right eyes overlap, so presumably they have partially stereoscopic vision. The sense of smell is, however, either non-existent or almost wholly so.

Hearing is the main sense, apart from taste and touch. This is acute and is especially sensitive to high tones. It is probably second only to the hearing of bats. A dolphin is sensitive to the pulses of an echo-sounder or asdic and will respond to frequencies as high as 120 kilocycles or beyond, whereas we can hear 30 kilocycles at the most. At sea it has been noticed that bottlenose dolphins will avoid a boat that has been used for hunting them but will not be disturbed by other boats. The assumption is that they can recognize individual boats by the sounds they make.

Feeding

Fish form one of the main items in the diet but a fair amount of cuttlefish is eaten, the dolphin spitting out the chalky cuttlebone and swallowing only the soft parts. Shrimps also are eaten. In captivity a bottlenose will eat 22 lb of fish a day, yielding 237 calories per pound of its body weight, compared with the 116 calories/lb taken by man.

Life history

Bottlenose dolphins become sexually mature

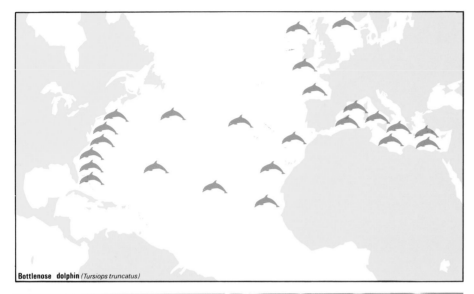

Bottlenose dolphin *(Tursiops truncatus)*

Peter Hill

Marineland Florida

△△ *Bottlenose dolphin jaws are well armed with teeth that help it catch its mainly cuttlefish food.*
△ *Baby dolphin with its mother. As with most mammals it stays with its mother for some time and is suckled on milk, being weaned after 5 months or more. Note the blowhole or nostril on top of the head.*

at 5—6 years. The breeding season extends from spring to summer. The gestation period is 11—12 months, births taking place mainly from March to May. The baby is born tail-first and as soon as free it rises to the surface to take a breath, often assisted by the mother usually using her snout to lift it gently up. Just prior to the birth the cow slows down and at the moment of birth she is accompanied by two other cows. These swim one either side of her, their role being protective, especially against sharks, who may be attracted to the spot by the smell of blood lost during the birth process. Weaning may take place between 6—18 months; reports vary considerably.

For the first 2 weeks the calf stays close beside the mother, being able to swim rapidly soon after birth. Then it begins to move away, even to chase fish, although quite ineffectively. However, it readily dashes back to its mother's side or to its 'aunt', the latter being another female that attaches herself to the mother and shares in the care of the calf. The aunt is the only one the mother allows near her offspring.

The calf is born with the teeth still embedded in the gums. These begin to erupt in the first weeks of life but the calf makes little attempt to chew until 5 months old and some take much longer before they attempt to swallow solid food. Even then there may be difficulties and in captivity a calf at about this time has been seen to bring up its first meal, the mother then massaging its belly with her snout.

Suckling is under water. The mother's nipples are small and each lies in a groove on the abdomen. The mother slows down to feed her calf which comes in behind her and lies slightly to one side, taking a nipple between its tongue and the palate. The mother then, by muscular pressure on the mammary glands, squirts the milk into its mouth. Should the calf let go the nipple the milk continues to squirt out. The baby bottlenose must come to the surface to breathe every half minute, so suckling must be rapid. In this species it consists of one to nine sucks, each lasting a few seconds. For the first 2 weeks the calf is suckled about twice an hour, night and day, but by 6 months it is down to six feeds a day.

Can dolphins talk?

It is not all that time ago that it was generally believed that whales, porpoises and dolphins were more or less mute, although the whalers themselves held views to the contrary (see beluga p. 332). It was not until after World War II, when bottlenose dolphins were being first kept in captivity in the large seaquaria, first in Florida and later in California and elsewhere, that it began to be realized fully that they have a wide vocabulary of sounds. Then, a few years ago, came the startling suggestion that these cetaceans might be capable of imitating human speech, even perhaps of being able to talk to people, in a sort of Donald Duck language in which words are 'gabbled' in a very high pitch. These high hopes do not seem to have been realized, but apart from this much has been learned about the noises they make.

One thing that has long been known is

that air can be released from the blowhole while the animal is still submerged. This can be seen, by direct observation, emerging as a stream of bubbles. It can be used to produce sounds, and part of the mechanism for it is the many small pouches around the exit from the blowhole which act as safety valves, preventing any inrush of water.

It has been known for some time that some cetaceans are attracted over long distances by the cries of their fellows in distress. Conversely, people have been calling the animals to them by using whistles emitting sounds similar to their calls. Pliny, the Roman naturalist of the first century AD, knew of this, and in modern times the people on the Black Sea coasts have continued to do this. Sir Arthur Grimble also left us an account of what he called porpoise calling in South Pacific Islands. He described how local peoples in this area would call the porpoises from a distance to the shore. These items indicate an acute sense of hearing in dolphins and porpoises and a potentiality for communication by sounds on their part.

Underwater microphones as well as more direct observations in the various seaquaria have established that these cetaceans use a wide range of sounds. These have been variously described as whistles, squawks, clicks, creaks, quacks and blats, singing notes and wailings. It has been found that two dolphins which have been companions will, if separated, call to each other, and that a calf separated from its mother will call to her. Dolphins trained to leap out of water for food have been heard to make sounds at their attendants.

These are, however, only the sounds audible to our ears, which can deal only with the lower frequencies. Much of dolphin language is in the ultrasonic range, and if they are able to understand what we are saying, as one investigator has somewhat unconvincingly suggested, they could be using their own vocalizations to call us by rude names without our knowing it!

It has often been said that if whales cried out in pain we might be less ready to slaughter them. Scattered reports suggest that in fact they do precisely this. Freshly captured bottlenose dolphins placed in the tanks in Florida's Marineland have been heard through the thick plate glass windows to cry with shrill notes of discomfort and alarm. At sea similar distress calls have been heard from injured or wounded whales, porpoises and dolphins.

class	**Mammalia**
order	**Cetacea**
family	**Delphinidae**
genus & species	***Tursiops truncatus***

Bottlenose dolphins leaping out of the water in formation. This demonstrates the powerful swimming action of the tail with its horizontal fluke unlike a fish's tailfin which is vertical. It also shows their sociability.

Peter Hill

Dolphins on the phone

Dolphins try to find each other by echo-locating 'clicks'. Then they talk in 'whistles' with a few 'grunts' and 'cracks'. Their sounds were analysed in 1965 when TG Lang and HAP Smith of the US Naval Ordnance Test Station put two newly captured bottlenose dolphins, Doris and Dash, in separate tanks linked by a two-way hydrophone system so the experimenters could tap their conversations. The first 4 of a total of 16 two-minute periods shown here indicate how the animals conversed when they were linked by phone and how sporadic noises were made when the line was 'dead'.

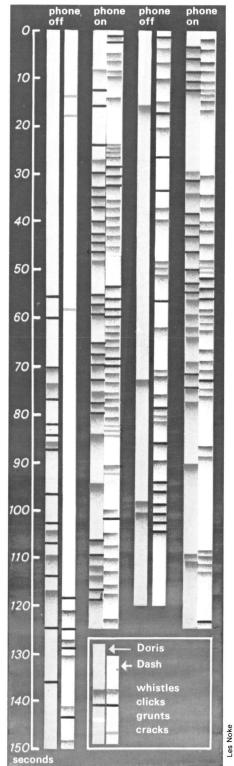

phone off   phone on   phone off   phone on

0
10
20
30
40
50
60
70
80
90
100
110
120
130
140
150
seconds

← Doris
← Dash

whistles
clicks
grunts
cracks

Les Noke

411

Bower-bird

*There are several species of bower-birds,
but the best-known and the one most
studied is the satin bower-bird of the coastal
forests of eastern Australia. The adult
male, about 1 ft long, is almost uniformly
black, but in the sunlight it appears a
beautiful lilac blue. The eye is also blue,
the precise shade varying with the bird's
changing emotions. Its legs are a dull
greenish-yellow and the beak is blue with
a greenish-yellow tip. The female satin
bower-bird is coloured quite differently.
Her head and back are blue-grey to olive-
green, varying with the light. Her underparts are olive, pale green and yellow.
In flight the brown wings show a yellow
patch with a grey border, and the brown
tail also shows some yellow. Her beak is
horn-coloured, and her legs and eyes are
like those of the male.*

Habits and life history

All that we know of the lives of bower-birds
is so intricately bound up with the building
of the bower that it is appropriate to give
it as one story, beginning with the young.

The young satin bower-birds have a plumage similar to that of the hen, but as the
young males mature, which they do at about
6 years old, the generally greenish plumage
changes to the dark dress of the fully adult
male. Before achieving this, however, the
growing males come into the breeding condition. That is, they mature sexually before
becoming fully adult. They then start making bowers which have given these and related birds their name. The first attempts
consist of collecting a small number of
sticks, some of which are laid on the ground
and others set vertically. Among the sticks
are placed decorative objects, such as
flowers, shells and feathers. The next year's
effort shows a considerable advance on this.
Much more material is collected and the
bower consists of a platform of sticks, with
a double fence of sticks set vertically in it.
The number of decorative objects will have
increased, also. With the third season, the
proportions of the bower increase in all
respects. The platform of sticks is larger,
the palisades longer, thicker and there is
much more decoration.

Instinctive builders

Bower building mainly follows an innate
behaviour pattern, but the full ability to
build takes several years to emerge. At
some time between April and September,
with a peak of building in July, each male
takes over a territory and constructs a
bower. The actual construction takes place
in a day or two, after which an area of
ground at one end of the bower, the display ground, is decorated with any available objects coloured blue, grey, brown,
yellow or greenish-yellow, the dominant
colours in the hen's plumage.

There may be 100 or more decorative
items including natural objects such as
feathers and flowers, fungi, wasp-nests, the
cast skins of snakes and shells of snails.
Near human habitations any scraps of

Graham Pizzey NHPA

△ *After decorating his maypole bower the bower-bird may step back, head cocked, to admire his work.*

△ *Greater bower-bird* Chlamydera nuchalis *displaying to female watching from the background.*
The display ground at both ends of the bower has been decorated with stones, twigs and pieces of bone.
◁ *Male satin bower-bird enticing female into his bower. After mating she will make a nest elsewhere.*
▽ *Male satin bower-bird building bower.*

John Warham

Pieces of coloured glass, bottle tops, buttons and string add variety to natural objects such as twigs, stones and snail shells used by this greater bower-bird to decorate his display ground.

Satin bowerbird
(Ptilonorhynchus violaceus)

materials of the same colour may be collected, such as paper, rags, broken glass or crockery, milk bottle tops, match-boxes, string, chocolate wrappers, and the like.

At first the main pre-occupation of the possessor of a bower is to keep other males away. He advertises his own presence by flying onto a nearby branch and calling loudly. The appearance of a rival male brings him flying down to the attack, usually no more than an aggressive feint, at which the intruder flees. In due course, a hen is brought to the bower and there the male displays to her. He picks up a blue feather, a brown snail shell or a sprig of yellow mimosa in his beak, lowers his head and stretches his neck, half opens his wings, fans his tail, his feathers glistening in the sunlight. At the same time he distends his eyes and makes a rhythmic whirring song.

The display may last a few seconds or half a minute; he may hop on stiff legs, run forward, pause, hop sideways, while the wings and tail flick rapidly. Meanwhile, the hen watches with more or less interest, at the most uttering a few low notes, starting now and then as the sun catches the male's plumage, or re-arranging a stick in the bower. Should she move away from the bower, he ceases his display and calls to her with a special double call, to which she normally responds by returning to her station near or in the bower. This is the course of events early in the season. Later, under the same circumstances, he interrupts his displays, re-arranges twigs in the bower with a peculiar sliding action of the neck, then follows the hen and leads her back to the bower.

Although the construction of the bower and its decor is so essentially a masculine affair, there are indications that the hen may have some slight abilities in this direction. She may re-arrange the twigs while the male is displaying or while he is away. And a hen in a cage next to a male displaying has been seen to bring coloured materials towards his display ground. Even so, the creative activities of the hen are almost entirely reserved for the building of a flimsy nest. She builds it well away from the bower and lays 1–3 eggs, incubating and feeding the chicks alone.

Painting and decorating

In addition to decoration with coloured objects, the walls of the bower may be painted with various pigments. These may be the juices of coloured berries, or charcoal from bush fires made into a liquid paste with saliva, or the contents of a washing-bluebag filched from a human habitation. A piece of fibrous bark is often used as a kind of swab for dabbing the colour onto the sticks of the bower. Not all the males of the satin bowerbird do this. On the other hand, some decorate the bower in this way every day during the height of the breeding season.

There are a number of species of bowerbirds, or related species, in Australia and New Guinea, each with its own methods of building. Some use, like the satin bowerbird, the avenue type of bower with parallel walls of sticks enclosing a central avenue. Others build what has been termed the maypole type, somewhat inappropriately, as the bowers are much more elaborate than any maypole. The simplest consists of the lower parts of a sapling decorated with twigs producing an effect similar to that seen in artificial Christmas trees. Elaborations of this lead to something very like a wigwam of twigs with a 'garden' in front sometimes bounded by a 'hedge' of twigs. The use of the term 'maypole' is appropriate only because around the Christmas-tree type, and in front of the wigwam type there is a display ground, which is more or less circular. The term 'maypole bower' is appropriate, however, in that it conjures up in our minds the old springtime rite of humans, of which the bower-bird's display is an exact parallel.

Birds as artists

Some people see in the bowers of these birds something akin to human arts and crafts. Certainly in the more elaborate maypole bowers the end result looks very like a house with garden in front bounded by a hedge and with flowers in the garden. There are similarities also in the way the male bower-bird will place a leaf or other object on or near the bower, step back, cock his head on one side, then come forward to pick up the object and place it somewhere else. He may continue to do this until, to

all appearances, he is satisfied that he has produced the best effect. Such a bird reminds one forcibly of the artist stepping back from his easel to survey his painting.

Students of animal behaviour have a less romantic explanation. They argue that in both male and female bird there is an impulse to build. In many species this results in both birds of a pair combining to build a nest. There are other species in which the male takes little or no part in making the nest. His creative impulses and energies are therefore channelled in other directions, in what is called 'displacement activity'. In the bower-birds the males build bowers. This, no doubt, is the correct explanation of basic causes, but the bower is definitely the outcome of a creative activity. Perhaps even human arts and crafts are due to a creative impulse, though differently expressed.

In the area in Australia where bowerbirds live is an Aborigine cemetery. The graves were once decorated with leaves, just as the bowers of the birds living in the neighbourhood are decorated. Then the white man's settlements encroached, and with them all manner of waste objects, such as tin-cans. The Aborigines, instead of renewing the decorations on the graves with fresh leaves, took to decorating them with tin-cans, broken crockery and such objects. This is surprisingly like the bower-birds living near human settlements, who take to decorating their bowers with match boxes, milk bottle tops and the rest.

If the male bower-bird's works are the result of a displacement activity, as has been claimed, it may also be true that human art has basically the same origin, an outlet for a creative urge that cannot be satisfied by any of the activities of everyday life.

class	**Aves**
order	**Passeriformes**
family	**Ptilonorhynchidae**
genus & species	*Ptilonorhynchus violaceus* *satin bower-bird, others*

Bowfin

The bowfin is a living fossil with many primitive features whose ancestors abounded 130 million years ago. A single species now occupies a family and an order on its own. It is a freshwater fish found only in the lakes and streams of the eastern United States, although its ancestors were widely distributed over North America and Europe, where their fossils may be found. Normally about 2 ft in length, it may reach 3 ft. Long-bodied, pike-like, it has a long soft-rayed dorsal fin, a rounded tail and thin scales with an enamel-like covering of ganoine. The head is covered with bony plates. The male has a dark spot circled with orange or yellow at the base of the tail fin. In the female it is either lacking or is merely a dark spot.

Voracious feeders

The bowfin eats crustaceans, worms, frogs and fishes, as well as dead flesh. It is so voracious and takes such a wide variety of animal foods that where the fish is abundant it is considered destructive and steps are taken to eradicate it. In the southern United States it is used as food, smoked or dried and in fishballs and jambalaya. Fishing for bowfins is said to be exciting sport because they will snap at almost any bait, although frogs and minnows are most used. Because the bowfin has strong jaws and sharp teeth which can tear its prey apart, it has also been called the freshwater dogfish or the freshwater wolf.

Male nests and guards the young

Spawning takes place in May to June, when the male's dark spot with its ring of colour becomes more intense. The male selects a weedy area along the margin of a lake or stream. There he builds a circular nest

What is a living fossil?

The bowfin is only one of many animals to have been called a 'living fossil'. This term was first used by Darwin for a tree, the ginkgo or maidenhair tree, which was worldwide in Mesozoic times 200 million years ago, when the giant reptiles roamed the earth, but was found by Europeans, in the 18th century, to be still surviving in China and Japan. It was about the same time, in the Mesozoic age, that large-mouthed predatory fishes first appeared. The family to which the bowfin belongs sprang from these and during the last 150 million years reached its zenith and then declined, the only species left being that now found in the eastern United States. Another species persisted in Europe until 50 million years ago and then died out. So this fish is a typical 'living fossil'; not a missing link but a link with the past. It has outlived its era and is the sole survivor from a past heyday.

John Tashjian at Vancouver Aquarium

Air breathing fish

The bowfin, mudfish, or spotfin is quite a remarkable fish which can breathe air. It lives in still waters and sluggish streams, and can survive in water with little or no oxygen. As with several other primitive fishes the swimbladder of the bowfin has a spongy inner lining well supplied with bloodvessels and acts as a lung, the bowfin rising to the surface to gulp air. It can live out of water for as much as 24 hours. It is said to utter a bell-like note which is possibly due to exhaling before taking in more air. Another primitive feature, which is more pronounced in sharks, is the spiral valve in the intestine. There is only a vestige of this valve in the bowfin, but even that is unusual in the bony or true fishes, to which the bowfin belongs. Another feature characteristic of primitive bony fishes is the large bony gular plate, on the underside of the head between the two lower jawbones. The bowfin swims mainly by a rapid wave-like motion of its long dorsal fin.

among a clump of water plants. He is said to swim round and round pressing the vegetation down, much as a bird fashions a nest by pivoting in it. Several females lay their eggs in the nest and the male, after fertilising these by shedding his milt on them, guards the nest until the eggs hatch, which they do in 8–10 days. The eggs stick to the stems and leaves of the plants. The guardian male, by swimming round and round the nest, creates currents that aerate the eggs. He also guards the young until they are about 4 in. long, when his parental instinct wanes. Such parental care behaviour is obviously an advantage for a species living in sluggish and poorly oxygenated water. The young fishes have their own protective device in the form of cement organs at the end of the snout. With these they can cling to water plants when first hatched and until their rapid growth makes them large enough and strong enough to swim, when they leave the nest in a compact group with the male in attendance.

△ *A living fossil, the bowfin is the sole surviving member of a family which flourished 130 million years ago. Even more remarkable, this large and fierce fish can breathe air and the male makes a nest and guards the eggs and babies.*

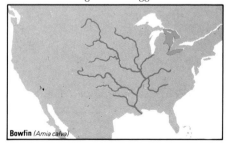

Bowfin *(Amia calva)*

class	**Osteichthyes**
order	**Protospondyli**
family	**Amiidae**
genus & species	*Amia calva*

BOXERS

Boxers are a breed of dog entirely designed by man, a product of the talent of the German nation for developing dog characteristics into new formulations. The first Boxer Club, founded in Munich in 1896, registered as Boxer No 1 a dog which was Brabanter Bullenbeisser on its dam's side, and had a pure English Bulldog as its sire. The breed, designed from the first to have cropped ears and a docked tail, therefore brought together all the attributes of the great Mastiff dogs of Europe whose ancestry goes back to our earliest recorded times. These were dogs with great jaws, power in the shoulders, enormous heart and enthusiasm for a fight, and these characteristics, in modified form and in a smaller package, are what we have in the Boxer today.

Guard instinct
The Boxer is a dog capable of inflicting great damage, on people or their possessions, while being capable of complete devotion and the utmost loving companionship. The guard instinct only becomes apparent when the dog is adult, at around two years old, but by that age it is inbuilt in every dog and bitch, however mild its bearing. Most Boxers are reserved with strangers, and their attack, when it comes, is quick and purposeful, delivered in complete silence and not preceded by barking. This guard instinct only flourishes where there is a bond of companionship between dog and owner, the Boxer will not guard unless it feels a sense of ownership.

Origin of the name
The origin of the name 'Boxer' has never

The drop-eared Boxer. Ear-cropping is not allowed in some countries.

been clearly established, but the favourite theory is that it refers to the dexterity with which these dogs wield their front paws and their evident liking for a friendly wrestle, or an all-out fight if they find it necessary.

Modern history
In Germany, the Von Dom kennel owned by Friedrun and Philip Stockman dominated Boxer breeding for many years and it was the stud dog Sigurd Von Dom, bought by Mr and Mrs Wagner's Tugley Wood Kennels, which set the seal of popularity on the Boxer

in America. Later, Mr Wagner bought the great Champion Lustig Von Dom and during World War II many good Boxers were sold in the USA. This blood, however, was very generously returned to Germany and Britain after the war through the gifts of puppies to leading breeders to enable them to start again.

Claustrophobic
The Boxer must be close to the people it loves. Many individuals in the breed are claustrophobic and will become destructive if shut away. Ideally they should always be with their owners and as many people are motorists it is often practical to let them assume their proper role as personal companion and guard, intensely loyal and totally devoted. As puppies, Boxers are great humourists, agile and a lot of fun as playmates for growing children, although they can be wonderfully gentle with babies and the old and weak. The Boxer has superb ability to adjust its behaviour to the mood of its owner, a characteristic cultivated by the steady watch it keeps on its owner's face, even when at rest. This breed, more than any other, seems to need physical closeness and tactile contact. They want to be touched, and to lie in bodily contact with their owners or rest with their fellow dogs in a great, gently snoring, fragrant heap.

Easily groomed
The short tight coat is easy to keep clean with the minimum of grooming. The hair is only shed twice a year but is extraordinarily adhesive. The coat colours are shades of brindle and fawn to red, with or without white markings on head, collar and paws. White puppies, or white with a small amount of coloured marking are usually discarded as they do not conform to the standard laid down by the Kennel Clubs of the world. The American standard states that males should be 22½ to 25 inches at the withers, females 21 to 23½ inches.

A mature Boxer male, with cropped ears. Boxers should be strong and muscular, but also elegant.

416

Bream

The name dates back to the 12th or 13th century and is said to be derived from a Teutonic word meaning to glitter. Its back is a dark blue-grey, often almost black, but the flanks are a gleaming dull silver. It is a stocky fish, strongly compressed, with a deep body, high arched back, especially in the older ones, and a small head. The lateral line, instead of following the curve of the back, follows the curve of the belly. It is a freshwater fish of the carp family living in Britain, chiefly in the east and south, and in continental Europe as well as Asia, from Turkestan to Siberia. Bream grow to about 2 ft in length and can weigh as much as 17 lb, although 10 lb would be considered a large fish.

The name bream has been given to another member of the carp family, the white or silver bream, of similar habits and appearance to the common bream. The young of the two species are difficult to tell apart. The adult white bream can be distinguished by, among other things, the red or orange tinge on the paired fins. Some marine fishes belonging to the families Sparidae (Porgies) and Labridae (Wrasses) are known as sea-breams.

Sluggish habits

Bream live in shoals. When about 3 in. long they frequent shallow water near the bank in still or slow-moving water, keeping to the bottom. In their second year they move into deep water, shunning the light, hiding in the mud and coming up into shallow water at night to feed. In winter bream rest at the bottom in deep water. They are always sluggish except at spawning time.

River bed feeders

The mouth is protractile and forms a sort of tube when shot out for feeding. Soon after hatching, young bream begin to feed on small plankton but later, when they move into shallow water near the bank, they seek bottom-living crustaceans, worms and small molluscs. In their second year, when they have moved to deeper water, they stir up the mud on the bottom with their snouts, feeding on organic matter in the mud and on insect larvae, worms, and molluscs. Larger bream eat similar food but also take small fishes.

Enemies

Young bream fall victim to the usual predatory fishes, but as they grow in size their deep bodies give them some protection from pike, for example. Their main protection lies, however, in their habits of keeping out of sight in deep water and in burying themselves in the mud. Their grubbing at the bottom sends up clouds of mud and streams of bubbles to the surface. The bream's vulnerable period, apart from infancy, is the breeding season, when prior to spawning they come to the surface, rolling and leaping.

Jane Burton: Photo Res.

This large freshwater fish is widely eaten in Europe where it is bred and reared on fish farms.

Life history

Male and female are alike but at spawning time from May to June, the female, swollen with eggs, looks more robust. The fishes come into shallow water, where there are plenty of water plants. Each female lays about 250,000 eggs which stick to the leaves and stems of water plants. In 2–3 weeks these hatch. After spawning, the adults go back into deep water. In any one place bream usually spawn in three groups: first the oldest and heaviest, a week later the medium-sized and a week after that the smaller, freshly adult individuals.

Fish and fashions

In Britain bream are not much fancied for the table but in the rest of Europe there is a well-established fishery for them. Indeed, except for salmon, trout and eel, river and lake fishes are unimportant as a source of food in Britain. This is not because such fishes have no food value; bream compare well with common food fishes as the table shows.

fish	% protein	% fat	calorific value
bream	16.19	4.09	473
halibut	18.6	5.2	565
haddock	17.2	0.3	335
cod	16.5	0.4	325

It is said that most freshwater fishes have a muddy flavour, but this can be eliminated by special methods of cooking. Yet only a few hundred tons are sold in Britain each year, supplied mainly by imports from Holland, where carp and other coarse fish are cultivated in an organized industry. Even this small amount is bought largely by European Jews and foreigners living in Britain.

But the British are not peculiar in failing to take advantage of a valuable food source. One of the biggest obstacles to making full use of natural food resources all over the world, especially of fish, is prejudice due to fashion. It is one of the problems that has to be faced now and in the future, in providing food for exploding human populations, but there are simpler examples to be seen nearer at hand. Dogfish, under that name would be unacceptable, but is readily eaten when labelled rock salmon. Redfish, abundant in the North Atlantic but marketed only recently, is readily eaten as fish fingers whereas had this fish with an unfamiliar name been offered directly it would almost certainly have been left unsold.

class	**Osteichthyes**
order	**Cypriniformes**
family	**Cyprinidae**
genus & species	***Abramis brama***

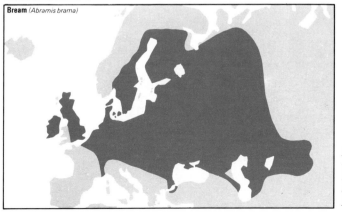

Bream *(Abramis brama)*

Bream live in slow-moving streams and lakes throughout much of northern and eastern Europe.

417

Brine shrimp

This is a small and primitive relative of crabs and lobsters, found in very salty water in many parts of the world, from Greenland to Australia and from the West Indies to Central Asia. In southern Europe, and formerly in England, it has been found in the shallow ponds where sea water has evaporated to produce a highly concentrated salt solution. There, though each shrimp is less than ½ in. long, it may be so abundant as to colour the water red. (The red colour is due to the red, oxygen-carrying pigment haemoglobin.)

The brine shrimp has two pairs of antennae, two compound eyes on stalks, and a third, small, eye in the middle of its head. It has 11 pairs of limbs. With the latter, it swims upside down — or rather with its ventral surface to the light, for it will turn over if illuminated from below (see p. 272).

The physical appearance of the animal varies a little with the amount of salt in the water in which it grew up. As a result some spurious species have been described. One of these, Artemia milhauseni, was exposed in 1875 when identical animals were produced from Artemia salina reared in a certain concentration of salt water.

Feeding as it swims

The brine shrimp feeds on the tiny particles of organic matter suspended in the water through which it swims. The rippling motion of the 11 pairs of flattened limbs, each one-sixth of a beat ahead of the pair in front, sweeps the particles in currents of water backwards along the front of the body. The particles are caught in strainers formed by the bristles on the inner edges of the limbs and are thence transferred forward to the mouth.

Males not essential

During reproduction the male brine shrimps clasp the females by means of specially modified antennae. The females have a brood pouch attached to the body behind the limbs, where the larvae remain for some time before being liberated when conditions are favourable to their survival. The young are active, with short bodies, no limbs, but large antennae, used for swimming. These so-called 'nauplius' larvae become adults after a succession of moults and, in a warm room, become mature in 3 weeks. Some colonies have females only and in these the eggs develop without being fertilised (parthenogenesis).

Sometimes, and as a result of mating and not parthenogenesis, eggs are laid that may either hatch very soon or lie quiescent for long periods. Such 'resting' eggs have hard brown shells and can be dried and kept for years before being hatched in salt water. Since many of the ponds and lakes in which brine shrimps live owe their extreme saltiness to the evaporation of water, and may sometimes dry up completely, the value of an egg that can survive the complete disappearance of water is obvious.

This is also very convenient for aquarists, who use brine shrimps as fish food. They buy the dry eggs and hatch out the larvae, rearing them to adulthood in seawater on a diet of yeast. The eggs they buy are packaged in various parts of North America,

Brine shrimp magnified 20 times. It occurs in various parts of Europe in salt lakes and marshes, where it can endure very high concentrations of salt. Some of its minor features change with the degree of salt concentration, so it has been described under different specific names.

JAL Cooke

△ *Organic food particles are swept towards the mouth by the rippling motion of the trunk limbs.*

▽ *Nauplius larva hatches from a stout-shelled egg. The egg can survive in dry mud for months.*

especially around the Great Salt Lake of Utah where they can be collected by the shovelful. This abundance of eggs is also used in North Africa where they are made into a paste and eaten with dates.

Life beyond boiling point

It is remarkable enough that the resting eggs should be able to survive for years when dried out, but this is not the limit of their tolerance. By drying them in a high vacuum, practically every trace of water can be removed and then the chemical processes of life are brought to a complete standstill. If such dried eggs are cooled to the temperature of liquid air, around $-190°$C/$-310°$F, they will still hatch when returned to salt water at a normal temperature. Moreover, provided they are fully dry, a small proportion will even survive for 2 hours a temperature of $105°$C/$221°$F. To be boiled and live is quite an achievement!

The adults, too, are unusual in their tolerance of harsh conditions, but in a different way. They can be found in water so full of salt that crystals form around the edge of the pool. Such water would contain about 30% of salt as compared with the $3\frac{1}{2}$% present in the sea. In the laboratory, on the other hand, they will survive in sea water diluted to only a tenth of its normal strength. Curiously, however, although they can live in the sea, they do not do so and in nature live only in water that is more than twice as salty, e.g. in salt pans or salt springs. The explanation seems to be that they would be very vulnerable to many kinds of predators in the sea and that they can flourish only in water too concentrated for these potential enemies to survive. Thus are they literally preserved in brine!

A problem facing all animals living in water containing concentrations of salts different from those in their body fluids is that of preserving a proper internal balance of water and salts. This is because the concentrations of each constituent in the body tend always to equalize with those outside. An animal living in fresh water has to prevent the salts from leaking out of its body and one living in concentrated salt solutions has to prevent too many salts flooding into its body. The brine shrimp has to keep its internal salt concentration lower than that of the surrounding brine, as low indeed as that of a freshwater animal, by absorbing salty water from its alimentary canal and expelling the surplus salt through special gill areas on its limbs. In devoting its energies to this, it need expend far less on escaping predators—few of whom can survive in the brine shrimps' rigorous environment.

phylum	**Arthropoda**
class	**Crustacea**
sub-class	**Branchiopoda**
order	**Anostraca**
genus & species	*Artemia salina*

419

Bristlemouth

Probably the commonest fishes in the ocean, bristlemouths, together with the lantern fishes and hatchet fishes, form the so-called Lilliputian fauna of the deep-sea, which make up 90% of all the deeper-dwelling oceanic fishes preying upon small planktonic animals. There are between 400 and 500 bristlemouths to the pound. Their eyes are small and there are rows of small light-organs (photophores) on the flanks. Some species are black, others pale-coloured, depending on the depths at which they live.

1 cm / 1/2 in

1 cm / 1/2 in.

Malcolm McGregor

Deep sea fragile form

With any deep sea animal the habits must be deduced, almost entirely, from individuals brought to the surface in nets. The bodies of bristlemouths are so fragile they look as if they have been beaten and tossed about by the time the net reaches the surface. Bristlemouths have only a vestigial swim-bladder, or hydrostatic organ and therefore cannot afford a heavy skeleton, since the weight of this would be greater than the 'lift' given by the gas of the swim-bladder and the fishes would tend to sink.

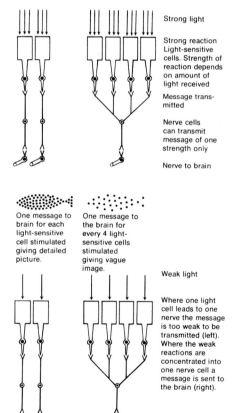

Strong light

Strong reaction Light-sensitive cells. Strength of reaction depends on amount of light received

Message transmitted

Nerve cells can transmit message of one strength only

Nerve to brain

One message to brain for each light-sensitive cell stimulated giving detailed picture.

One message to the brain for every 4 light-sensitive cells stimulated giving vague image.

Weak light

Where one light cell leads to one nerve the message is too weak to be transmitted (left). Where the weak reactions are concentrated into one nerve cell a message is sent to the brain (right).

Light-sensitive cells are found in the eye retina. Whether messages pass to the brain depends on the light strength and how the light cells are linked to nerve cells. Some bristlemouths have several light cells linked to one cell (bottom right) so they can see in dim light.

Bristlemouths are very common at depths over 1 500 ft, where they feed on copepods, amphipods and sea-butterflies which are picked off as they drift by. Although they look as if they could swim well this is not the case. They have a vestigial swim-bladder, or hydrostatic organ, and cannot afford a heavy skeleton, since the

So we find the skeleton is flimsy and soft rather than bony, except for the jaws. The muscles are correspondingly light. It is assumed, therefore, that bristlemouths do not swim quickly, and probably show little activity.

Large gape for small fish

Bristlemouths can open their mouths, armed with bristle-like teeth, through nearly 180°, a large gape for so small a fish. Despite this, they feed on copepods and other small planktonic animals such as amphipods and pteropods (sea-butterflies, p. 2173) picked off as they drift by. This much can be deduced from what is known of their habits, from their inactivity, and from an examination of their stomach contents. The problem then remains, since their eyes are small, as to how they detect their food.

Eyes may be large or small and may be adapted either for sharpness of vision in good light, or for making the maximum use of a small amount of light, at the same time sacrificing the ability to see detail. In the second type, the pupil needs to be large, with a large lens. Greater efficiency is achieved with a retina composed of very long cells which present more light-sensitive molecules to the rays of light entering the eye. The efficiency is further increased by several of these long cells being served by individual nerve-cells. This means they are equipped to make the most use of the little available light, although they cannot see much detail.

When a light-sensitive tube is lowered into the ocean, flashes of light can be detected even as far down as 13 000 ft whereas the penetration of sunlight ceases at depths between 1 500 and 1 800 ft. This comes from the light-organs of deep sea animals. But it is intermittent and sporadic and would provide a poor 'target' for feeding fish. We know that sources of odours and disturbances can be detected at a distance through the nose and the lateral line organs of fish. Presumably, therefore, bristlemouths do not hunt by sight, but by smell or by picking up minute vibrations in the water.

weight of a heavy skeleton would be greater than the 'lift' given by the gas of the swim-bladder and the fishes would tend to sink. So the skeleton is found to be flimsy and soft rather than bony, except for the jaws. The muscles are also light. This suggests that bristlemouths are slow and inactive.

Deep sea predators

Apart from the study of bristlemouths brought up in the nets, the only source of information is the stomach contents of deep sea predatory fish captured in hauls for scientific purposes. Many bristlemouths are found in their stomachs.

The rising eggs

The eggs are laid in deep waters and then rise to the surface layers, where they hatch. The larvae are massed in the upper waters throughout spring and summer, the adolescents and adults occupying different levels in the sea.

No room for competition

The density of plankton is greatest in the shallow waters, yet in the deep waters live the most numerous fishes in the world. There are many species of them, and each can flourish by avoiding competition with the others, by living at different depths. However, they do not fully achieve this, and in doing so provide a striking example of a basic law: that if in a balanced community of organisms, two species occupy the same living space one is bound to become dominant. In the 1920's and 1930's a group of scientists, led by the American, William Beebe, made 1 500 net hauls to the south of Bermuda over a period of nine years. Among the fishes taken were two related species of *Cyclothone, C. microdon* and *C. pallida*, but whereas they caught 57 512 *C. microdon*, only 505 *C. pallida* were taken. *C. pallida* was outnumbered by more than 113 to 1!

class	**Osteichthyes**
order	**Salmoniformes**
family	**Gonostomatidae**
genera & species	***Cyclothone microdon*** ***C. pallida***

The silverfish is often seen in kitchen cupboards. Looking like a small land fish it is really a wingless insect and has probably remained unchanged for 400 million years. It will eat anything from crumbs on the floor to the paste on the back of wallpaper, but it rarely becomes a pest.

Bristletail

Although bristletails live throughout the world, the silverfish, found in bread or flour bins, in larders, kitchens or pantries, behind skirtings, in cupboards or among books, is the only one of these small wingless insects which is at all well-known. They get their name from the three slender bristle-like 'tails', and their antennae also are long and bristle-like but no bristletail is more than 1 in. long overall. They have small compound eyes. Their legs are long and slender, well adapted for running.

In places they may sometimes be a pest, but usually they are not more than little noticed scavengers.

Nocturnal habits

If a bristletail finds itself in the light it will scamper rapidly into cover. This strong reaction to get away from light and their need to keep their bodies from drying out means that most bristletails live in damp sheltered places: under stones or logs, among leaf litter, under dead bark. Some live in the nests of ants and termites. They come out mainly by night, and this nocturnal habit combined with their small size and neutrally coloured slender bodies, means they are seldom seen. Those most commonly seen are two that have taken to living in houses, the silverfish, already mentioned, and the firebrat, so-named because it lives around fireplaces, boilers and flues. In fact, it was given its name by bakers because it was often seen around bakehouse ovens.

Scavenging feeders

All bristletails feed on bits of dead plant or plant products, ranging from particles of dead leaves to flour or anything containing starch. Silverfish will attack crumbs on the floor and they may eat paste from the back of wallpaper, where it has come away from the wall. They may also damage book-bindings, eating the paste. There are records of silverfish damaging artificial fabrics, but this is only when the materials have been treated with a natural plant extract.

Nymphs lack silvery scales

The female silverfish lays 7–12 eggs. These are minute and very hard to find as they lie freely on the ground where they are laid. They hatch in 6–60 or more days, depending on the temperature. The young silverfish, known as nymphs, resemble the adults in all but size and in lacking scales—the adult silverfish body is coated with silvery scales which come away readily, as a powder, when handled. Silverfish moult several times during the 20 months or more which they take to reach maturity.

The female firebrat lays a large number of eggs but otherwise follows much the same course in development.

Enemies

Little is known about enemies but it is assumed that bristletails are attacked by carnivorous insects, centipedes, spiders and other small predatory invertebrates.

Ancient ancestors

It is not surprising the silverfish should not be readily recognized as an insect. It was, in fact, given the name of silverfish at least as long ago as 1703, and it was not called a bristletail until 1855, when people had begun to study insects in an organized way. It looks more like a minute land fish. To begin with it does not obviously have the body in three parts, the hallmark of an insect, and it has no metamorphosis, the newly-hatched young looking very like the parents.

It had long been presumed that silverfish, and other wingless insects like it, represent an ancestral form of all the insects. This is on the supposition that they never did have wings, unlike other insect pests such as fleas and lice, whose ancestors were winged originally but later gave up flight for a parasitic way of life.

Until 20 years ago this view about the silverfish was largely hypothetical, for the only fossils to compare with it were silverfish found in amber and a mere 40 million years old, long after fully winged insects had evolved. Then insect remains were found in rocks of the Triassic, nearly 200 million years old. These were very like the silverfish living today. The earliest insect fossils known, also of wingless insects but of a different kind, are twice that age, and we can expect that sooner or later fossil bristletails 400 million years old, or more, will come to light.

phylum	**Arthropoda**
class	**Insecta**
order	**Thysanura**
family	**Lepismatidae**
genera & species	*Lepisma saccharina* silverfish *Thermobia domestica* firebrat others

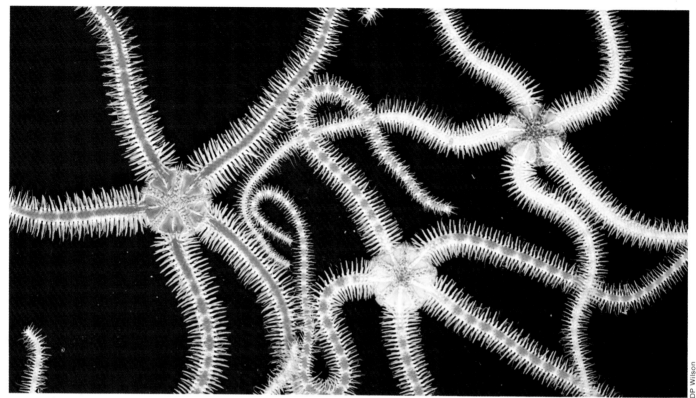

In some places, the floor of the English Channel is carpeted with masses of common brittlestars, Ophiothrix fragilis. *These are shown here at about the size of the largest specimens, but they are usually half this size. The name refers to the ease with which the arms fall off when handled.*

Brittlestar

These are echinoderms closely related to the basket stars (see p. 298) and more distantly related to the starfish. Like the latter, they have five arms joined to a central body, although some species may have more arms. The body, or disc as it is known, is button-shaped, and the arms are snake-like, hence the scientific class name of Ophiuroidea from the Greek ophis, serpent. The English name alludes to the ease with which the arms fall off. Any that do come off are regrown.

Some brittlestars are a light grey in colour but many are delicately coloured. The largest brittlestars have discs of 4 in. diameter with a spread of 2 ft across the arms. Another has a disc only ½ mm across.

The arms are covered with rows of hard plates and spines, while running down their centres are 'vertebrae' forming a flexible structure very much like our backbone. Muscles controlling movement are attached to these vertebrae. Along the underside of the arms are rows of tube-feet, or podia. These are badly named as they are used for feeding. Similar structures in starfish are used for walking.

Submarine acrobats

Brittlestars are found in seas all over the world from the tideline to deep water. One species is almost cosmopolitan, being found off the shores of Europe and New Zealand and on both east and west coasts of America.

Many species of brittlestar live on the seabed, burrowing into it if it is muddy.

Others live amongst seaweeds and corals, climbing around the fronds by grasping them with their flexible arms rather like a monkey swings through the trees. On the seabed they move by waving the arms in a rowing action. Either two or four arms work together in pairs. The fifth is held out in front or trails behind, sometimes assisting in the motion by a beating action. By this means brittlestars can travel at speeds of as much as 2 yd/min, which is quite fast compared with the slow crawls of other echinoderms such as starfish or urchins which drift along on their tube-feet.

Two ways of feeding

Brittlestars have two basic feeding methods. They capture small particles on the arms, which are then passed to the mouth that lies on the underside of the disc, or they tear off lumps of dead flesh or seaweed with the tube-feet and teeth around the mouth.

Collecting small particles is a passive method of feeding. The brittlestar rests on the seabed or burrows down into the mud, leaving only the arms from which long sticky mucous threads wave about in the water. Organic debris in the mud or floating in suspension, as well as minute planktonic animals and plants, are trapped in the mucus.

The skin around the arms is covered with cilia (protoplasmic hairs) which sweep the mucus and the entrapped particles in towards the tube-feet on the underside of the arms. The tube-feet also help in this movement by 'licking' around the parts of the arm within reach. In this way they become covered in a mixture of mucus and particles. This is then wiped off against a spine near each one and the resulting mass transferred on the tip of the tube-foot to another nearer

the mouth. As the mass is moved inwards more is added and it is patted by the tube-feet to form a compact ball. Eventually it is brought to the root of the arm, where it is transferred to tube-feet around the mouth. These taste the ball and, if it is acceptable, they force it into the mouth. If unpalatable, they reject it, pushing it back onto the arm. It is then passed back down the arm and released to drift away.

Brittlestars also feed on larger animals or carrion. Large lumps of food, up to 1 in. across are caught, wrapped in an arm and held by the tube-feet. The arm then curves over to carry the food to the mouth. Smaller lumps are grasped by the arm then transferred along it by the tube-feet in the same way as the mucous ball. Lumps of food still smaller are merely grasped by the tube-feet without the arms flexing over to hold them.

Brittlestars can detect the presence of food, provided it is upstream of them, presumably by 'tasting' chemicals liberated from the food. The arms wave about, then, having found out in which direction the food lies, the brittlestar moves towards it.

Simple sexual organs

In most species, eggs and sperms are merely shed into the sea, where fertilisation takes place. The sexual organs are, therefore very simple. There are genital openings at the base of each arm through which the sex cells are discharged. There may, however, be a bag, or bursa, just inside the slit, into which the cells are discharged from the gonads.

The fertilised eggs develop into delicate larvae with long arms, stiffened with fine rods, and covered with cilia whose beating keeps the larva from sinking. The larva is called an *ophiopluteus*, *pluteus* meaning easel-like, an apt description. After floating about for some time, the larva develops into the adult form and settles on the seabed.

A few brittlestars do not have free-swimming larvae but retain their eggs in the bursae or in the ovaries, where they develop into small adults before crawling out through the genital slits. These species are often hermaphrodite, having both male and female sex organs, but they avoid self fertilisation by the cells of one sex ripening before the other.

Lost arms replaced

Brittlestars fall a prey to fish such as plaice and dab, that feed on the sea bottom. The species that burrow into the mud avoid predation to some extent, apart from having their arms bitten off which is of no great importance as the arms are readily regrown.

Some brittlestars have light-producing cells on the spines of the arms and when one arm is bitten off, the others produce a flash of light as the brittlestar withdraws. This, presumably, deters the predator from following up the attack (and may even put it off attacking any more brittlestars).

Brittlestars cling together

Around the shores of the eastern coast of the United States there is a brittlestar that normally lives amongst the stems of eelgrass, hanging onto them by its arms. In winter the eelgrass dies back and the brittlestars twine their arms around each other to form a tight bunch. This habit has been examined in the laboratory. Whenever they are deprived of eelgrass the brittlestars bunch together, but it has been found that if vertical glass rods are placed in the aquarium, the brittlestars treat them as substitute eelgrass and twine their arms around them.

It seems, then, that the brittlestars have some need to twine around something and when there is no eelgrass or artificial substitute they will cling to each other. This contrasts with the usual gatherings of animals which are normally only for breeding or feeding.

The bunches form by random movements of the individuals, the more active ones clinging to the inactive ones, reacting to them as if they were a piece of glass or eelgrass. When gathered together, the bunch is drawn tighter and tighter. Brittlestars in bunches live longer than isolated ones and they are less likely to shed their arms. When curled around an object a brittlestar is exerting tension and the rate at which its body functions work goes up. For some reason that is not properly understood, this enables them to live longer. Therefore it is an advantage to cling to any object, so, without the normal solid supports, they cling to each other.

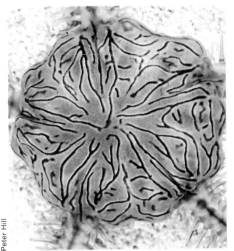

△ *Central disc of brittlestar magnified 12 times.*

▽ *The star-shaped mouth is on the underside.*

△ *Closeup of mouth, armed with spines serving as teeth, which leads directly into the stomach.*

phylum	**Echinodermata**
class	**Ophiuroidea**
order	**Ophiurae**
genera	**Ophiura, Ophiothrix, Amphiura,** *others*

Broadbill

Broadbills are brightly coloured with usually green or blue silky plumage. The long-tailed broadbill has a green body with a black and yellow head and blue on the crown, wings and tail. The three green broadbills seem to have minute bills but this is because the bill is covered with a tuft of small feathers. The 14 species of broadbill are plump birds, 5—11 in. long, with short legs and wide, hooked bills. The females are less brightly coloured than the males.

Broadbills live in wet jungles and forests of the tropics, especially the secondary forests where the virgin jungle has been burnt down and cultivated, then allowed to grow again. Some species live in mangrove swamps, gardens or fields. Most are found in south-east Asia from the Himalayan foothills to Borneo.

Noisy jungle flocks

Some broadbills live near the ground and others in the tree-tops, working through the forest in small flocks of up to 20, exploring branches and creepers, climbing about them like tiny parrots and continually calling and whistling to each other. Others, such as the green broadbills, are solitary and more silent.

The gregarious broadbills are well-known for their unusual tameness. They are unwilling to take flight even when one of them has been shot, in fact they tend to stay still rather than fly when alarmed.

Insects, lizards or fruit for food

Many broadbills are insect-eaters, probing into bark or pulling insects out of crevices. Flying insects are caught on the wing. The long-tailed broadbill feeds on large moths, stick insects and similar creatures, and the larger broadbills will take small lizards and frogs. The green broadbills eat mainly fruit.

'Sings' with its wings

At the beginning of the breeding season the small flocks of broadbills separate into pairs. Several species have elaborate courtship displays and there is a variety of songs within the family. The red-sided broadbill of Africa is called the 'cock of the forest' by the Congolese because it is the first bird to start singing in the morning. It makes short flights in a circle, only a foot or two in diameter, just above its perch. During this flight the bright red patches under the wings are displayed to attract the female, while a klaxon-like croak is made by the beating of the stiff wing feathers. Other species also make noises with their wings, or have musical, whistling songs.

The nest is a huge elaborate structure hanging from a branch, often over water. It is a pear-shaped mass of dead leaves, grass, sticks and fibres, perhaps 5—6 ft long and hanging about 10 ft above the ground, the height depending on the species that built it. The main bulk of the nest, hung

Longtailed broadbill carrying moth to its young waiting in the 3 ft long pear-shaped nest.

by a thin 'rope' of fibres and grasses, is intricately woven with an entrance in one side near the bottom and sometimes a porch or doorstep is added. Mosses and lichens decorate the exterior. Both sexes help in building the nest and in the dusky broadbill as many as ten individuals have been seen building one nest. Whether this is a sign of communal breeding, where all the females lay in the single nest, is not known.

As is usual with birds of the dense tropical forests, little is known of their breeding habits. They may lay from 2—8 eggs, but 3—5 is more usual. These are white or pinkish with a varying amount of purplish or red spotting. The length of the incubation period and the share taken by each sex is not known, but both parents have been seen feeding the young.

Lucky finds

Not only are the habits of jungle birds not well known, but in some cases the bird itself is hardly ever seen, for even common birds may escape detection if they are secretive.

One broadbill is known only from 12 specimens. It was first found by a collector called Rudolf Grauer in a bamboo forest north of Lake Tanganyika. In 1909 Lord Rothschild published a description of it, calling it *Pseudocalyptomena graueri* and attracting considerable interest in the ornithological world because, previously, broadbills were not thought to exist in Africa.

Another 20 years passed before it was seen again. Eventually Alan Moses, a member of an American expedition, tried to find it in the bamboo forests of Central Africa. He searched high and low without catching a glimpse of it and eventually he gave up, having convinced himself that it no longer existed. Having given up the search Alan Moses then climbed farther up, out of the bamboo forest into open, canyon-scarred country. After climbing some way he sat down to rest and, looking up, saw a small bird in the branches above. It was *Pseudocalyptomena graueri*. Imagine his excitement. It must have been the ornithologist's equivalent of a prospector finding a vein of gold or the art collector's discovery of an old master in an attic. But

in his haste to secure this rare specimen, Moses missed his target. Luckily, others were found up in the open country, not in the bamboo country where Rudolf Grauer must have found a wanderer, out of its habitat.

class	**Aves**
order	**Passeriformes**
family	**Eurylaimidae**
genera & species	**Calyptomena** *green broadbill* **Pseudocalyptomena graueri** *Grauer's broadbill* **Psarisomus dalhousiae** *longtailed broadbill* **Smithornis rufolateralis** *red-sided broadbill* **Corydon sumatranus** *dusky broadbill others*

Malayan green broadbill showing its small bill covered at the base with a dense tuft of fine feathers. It feeds on insects caught in flight.

Jane Burton: Photo Res.

Brown bear

It is a matter of opinion, almost a matter of taste, whether there are many species of brown bears distributed over Europe, Asia and North America, or whether there is only one. Authoritative writers are tending more to the view that the grizzlies and other brown bears of North America, such as the giant Kodiak and Kenai bears, belong to the same species as the European, Russian and Syrian bears, together with the isabelline bear of Central Asia. If we take this view, then the brown bear can be described as a heavily built member of the Carnivora, practically tailless, with broad flat feet, each foot bearing five toes armed with non-retractile claws. Its sense of sight is poor, but smell and hearing are acute. It may be up to 9 ft or more long and weigh up to 1 650 lb. Its coat is usually a shade of brown, but that of the isabelline bear is reddish.

The blue or snow bear, of western China and Tibet, has blackish-brown hairs frosted with slate-grey or silver.

Grizzly's great strength

Brown bears live in wild mountainous country, as well as forests, wandering about singly or in family parties. Their home range averages over a 20 mile radius, and individuals often stray beyond this. The wandering has been shown by finding bear tracks in the snow up one side of a mountain in Canada with a track down the other side where a bear had tobogganed down. They normally walk on all-fours but will at times stand erect and shuffle for a few paces. The dancing bears of former times, led through the streets on a chain with a ring through the nose, were trained to do this to order. Young brown bears climb trees well, though slowly and deliberately, but adults rarely do so. Brown bears are not normally aggressive to man except under provocation or when injured, or when a person comes between a she-bear and her

Brown bear
(Ursus arctos, U. horribilis, others)

△ Brown bear head. Scents play an important part in the social and family groups of carnivores. A good sense of smell is therefore very important. The bear has a well-developed snout with a wet nose, or rhinarium, which increases its sense of smell.

▽ Mother with her cub. When young, the bear can climb, but as it grows older this ability is lost. The cub is born in January or February while the mother is in her winter sleep. It weighs under 1½ lb at birth but by the time it is a year old it weighs about 50 lb.

cub. The strength of a bear can be shown by the grizzly's ability to fell a bison larger than itself with one blow of its paw, breaking its neck, and then dragging away the carcase. Bears feed during summer and store fat in their bodies then den up to sleep most of the winter in natural shelters among rocks or in a large hollow tree, even in dens dug in hillsides.

Omnivorous carnivore
Considering that bears are classified in the order Carnivora (flesh-eaters), it is perhaps surprising to find the diet varies greatly with the individual. Some bears are wholly vegetarian, others wholly flesh-eating, but most eat a mixture of plant and animal food. This is made up of berries and fruits, insects and other small animals, honey and the grubs of wild bees. Fish may be taken, flipped from the shallows onto the bank with the forepaws, or seized in the water, as in the salmon runs of western North America. Sometimes the young of deer are killed and eaten, and occasionally a rogue individual takes to killing farmstock.

Life history
This is similar to that of the black bear (see page 361). Mating is in June, the gestation period varies from 180–250 days, and the cubs, normally two, are born in January or February, while the mother is in her winter sleep. Each cub is 1–1½ lb at birth and 8 in. long, almost hairless, blind and toothless. The small size compared with the bulk of the mother is striking and an ancient belief was that they were born shapeless and that the mother 'licked them into shape', hence the well-known saying. The reference here is to the licking the mother gives each cub after birth to clean them, as in most true mammals, of the birth fluids. The mother rouses herself from her dozing sleep to do so. The brown bear cub weighs 54 lb when a year old, and stays with the mother until at least that age. Females may breed at three years. They live for up to 34 years.

Wiping out several species with a pen

Half-a-dozen species of brown bears, as well as many subspecies, have been recognized in the past. Over 50 species of grizzly alone have been named, as well as a number of subspecies. In Europe and Asia the position has been only a little better. Clearly this is absurd, especially as all have the same habitat, habits and life history as well as skeletons and general anatomy that are not significantly different. The truth is that this enormous list of species and subspecies was based mainly on different colours of the coat, a most variable feature in any mammal, and especially on differences in size. It is true that there is a big gap between the Syrian bear at 150 lb and the Kenai and Kodiak bears at 1 650 lb. The Syrian bear is the one usually seen in zoos in Britain so the mammoth proportions of the Kenai and Kodiak bears can be imagined. Even the grizzly, scientifically named *Ursus horribilis* (horrible bear), only reaches 880 lb.

It is more likely that the truth about these many species arises from two circumstances:

CJ Ott: Photo Res.

persecution and the absence of reliable records. In the Old World, brown bears once ranged in considerable numbers from Britain to Japan, and as far south as the Mediterranean and the Himalayas. By the 11th century the last had been killed in Britain and today, in Europe, the survivors are largely confined to inaccessible forests in the Pyrenees, Swiss Alps, Carpathians, Balkans, Norway, Sweden and Finland. They are more numerous in parts of the Soviet Union but even there numbers have dropped. It is self-evident that persecution, especially hunting, brings down radically the maximum sizes reached in a species, particularly when the hunters' ambition is to collect record trophies. Bears were killed for their flesh, and their fat, and because their tempers were unpredictable. Above all, their shaggy coats were coveted prizes, and this alone gave a large bear little chance.

In 1904 JG Millais, naturalist and author, wrote: 'No terrestrial mammal varies so greatly, both in size and pelage, as this animal. Between brown bears killed in eastern Norway and those of western Sweden there is a perceptible difference in colour, whilst in the bears of Russia, especially those of the eastern districts, there is a further and much greater difference in size. I have lately seen two enormous bears belonging to the Russian Embassy in London, which measure nearly 9 ft in length (the size of Kenai and Kodiak bears) and are almost black in colour.'

In Germany there are many so-called dragons' caves, including the Drachenfels, in the Sieben Gebirge, where Siegfried is supposed to have killed his dragon. The basis for these legends was the abundance of skulls of cave bears, larger than those of brown bears and characterised by a steeply sloping forehead. Nevertheless, the two bears were often confused until the years 1920-3 when Austria was in such a calamitous state economically. The loss of her cattle during the First World War caused an acute need for fertilizers. These were eventually found in caves, in the thick deposits of guano laid down by bats over the years. In the course of digging out the guano they found thousands of bones of bears, enabling scientists to build up a complete picture of the cave bear and of the modern brown bear that replaced it. The cave bear was larger, almost completely vegetarian, and it went into caves only for its winter sleep. This was clear from the large proportion of baby skeletons found under the bat guano. The study of the bones also revealed that many of the cave drawings until then believed to be of cave bears were, in reality, drawings of the living brown bear. The stratification of the bones in the guano showed that cave bears had died out before most cave drawings had been made.

class	**Mammalia**
order	**Carnivora**
family	**Ursidae**
genus & species	***Ursus arctos*** *brown bear*

◁ *Alaskan grizzly scratching his back.*

Brush-tail possum

The most common and most widely distributed of all species of Australian marsupials. It is found in all parts of Australia and Tasmania, and it flourishes in New Zealand, where it was introduced in 1858. The brush-tail possum, also known as the vulpine or fox-like possum, is about 2 ft long, the size of the red fox, has a fox-like head with large ears and a pointed snout. Its eye-catching feature, however, is its tail, which is prehensile at the tip where there is a naked patch on the underside. Its fur is thick, woolly and variable in colour, from silver-grey to dark brown or black.

Adaptable Australian

The brush-tail prefers trees but it will also live in the low bush or in treeless areas, where it will take over rabbit burrows. It has also taken to living in the roof-spaces of houses, even in the suburbs of large towns. Because it is nocturnal, the noise of the brush-tail moving in roof-spaces is unwelcome. So are the stains on the ceiling immediately under the roof. It also damages garden blossoms.

The brush-tail is indifferent to human beings. A wild one visiting the vicinity of houses has allowed itself to be stroked, although it objected to being picked up. It then attempted to bite and scratch although uttering no sound. This contrasts with the noise made in quarrels with its fellows, when it hisses and grunts, and follows with a loud cry which ends in a raucous screech.

Taste for mistletoe

It is largely vegetarian, feeding mainly on buds, and a preferred food is the Australian mistletoe. It is reputed to take eggs and nestling birds, and to eat carrion.

The lizard menace

A brush-tail abroad by day is likely to fall prey to eagles. So also is one with inadequate sleeping shelter, which means that the numbers of brush-tails in an area will be largely controlled by the availability of hollow trees or burrows. Dingoes try to hunt them, and will tear bark from a tree base to reach one. The main enemy is the monitor lizard known as the goanna. As this climbs a tree the brush-tail cries out in fear. The Aborigines, who cook and eat the brush-tail, imitate the goanna's scratching on the bark of a tree to find out if one is inside.

Born climber

Mating takes place in May–June, earlier in southern parts. Gestation is 17–18 days. There is a single young (possibly sometimes two) and this leaves the pouch in July–September, becoming independent of the mother by September–November. At birth it is $\frac{1}{2}$ in. long and weighs less than 1/15 oz, compared with the mother's weight of about 10 lb. It reaches full-size by the following February, and attains sexual maturity three months or so later.

The brush-tail, with its fox-like head, hangs in a bat-like position by its prehensile tail.

Australian News & Information Bureau: Photo Res.

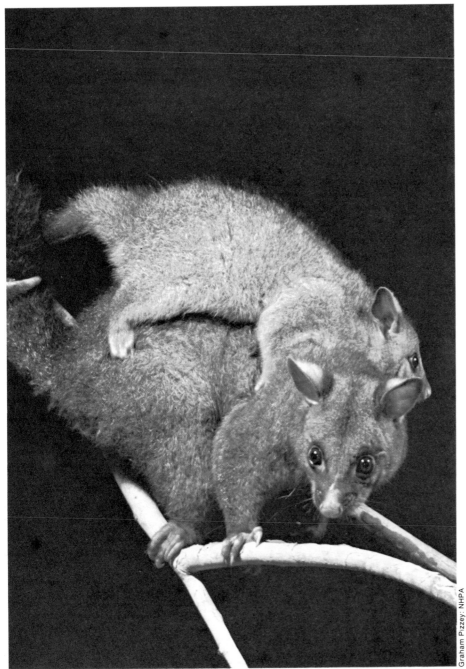

As with other baby marsupials, the newly-born brush-tail makes its way unaided from the birth-canal to the pouch through the mother's fur. It progresses by an over-arm action of the front legs, which at birth are longer than the hind-legs, the paws being armed with strong claws. The paws can be flexed to grasp the mother's fur. It takes the newly-born brush-tail about 7 minutes to travel the 2½ in. to the pouch. Once inside the pouch the baby seizes one of the two teats in its mouth and hangs on in this way for some weeks, by which time it is beginning to look more like its parents.

Should the baby fail to reach the pouch, or be lost through some other cause, a second will be born fairly soon.

Secrets of survival

The brush-tail population in New Zealand has reached the astonishing number of 25 million. Its only predator, however, is man. About 1 million a year are trapped for their fur and 1 million destroyed under a bounty system. There is an annual increase, despite these losses, of some 25% and this is despite the low birth-rate.

In Australia there are natural predators, but there is the same story of a successful survival despite persecution. The brush-tail is regarded as a pest in orchards and on farms. Moreover, there is continual attrition because of its valuable fur, which has been marketed and exported, and sold under such names as beaver, skunk and Adelaide chinchilla.

During the depression of 1931, unemployed men were encouraged to hunt the brush-tail for its fur. Between June and July of that year over 800 000 skins were marketed from crown lands alone. Previously, in 1906, over 4 million skins were sold in London and New York. The annual toll is not always of that order, and in most years is considerably less.

A more sympathetic attitude is growing, based partly upon the increasing realization of the need for conserving Australia's unique fauna. More particularly, also, is the realization that the brush-tail by feeding on the mistletoe, and thus checking its spread, is not only benefiting the indigenous trees but indirectly helping the honey industry. The economic value of this marsupial in reducing the prejudicial effect of the mistletoe on the flowering gum-trees, which produce the nectar for honey, has been proven by direct experiment.

There is almost certainly, as is so often the case, a need for local control. Given that, there is little to fear, for the brush-tail's ability to survive even under persecution is due, as in the common rat, to its adaptability. It can live in any kind of habitat and, being primarily a vegetarian, it is unlikely to suffer a shortage of food.

△ *Mother and baby coppery brush-tail possum.*
▽ *The brush-tail has invaded suburbs of towns.*

▽ *The vegetarian diet consists mainly of buds, and it has a taste for Australian mistletoe.*

class	**Mammalia**
order	**Marsupialia**
family	**Phalangeridae**
genus & species	*Trichosurus vulpecula*

A tree full of budgerigars in the Australian scrub is a wonderful sight. The large flocks are nomadic. With no fixed territories outside the breeding season, they move from one feeding ground to another. With the spread of agriculture, budgerigars have taken to eating grain.

Budgerigar

The commonest member of the parrot family in Australia, a continent already remarkable for the number and diversity of its cockatoos and parakeets. It is about 7 in. long, generally greenish, and swarms in millions in the arid parts of the continent. The aboriginal name is betcherrygah, said to mean 'good food', so it may be presumed the Aborigines have been eating them for a long time without making any impact on their numbers. An accepted Australian spelling of the name is budgerygah.

The wild budgerigar is grass-green with bright yellow on the head and a long tapering blue tail. The upper parts are barred and scalloped with black and yellow, there is a royal blue patch on each cheek and three black spots on each side of the throat. The male differs from the female in having the base of the bill blue instead of brownish.

The first budgerigars were brought to England in 1840. Since then, large numbers have been exported from Australia, and many more have been bred in captivity. By selective breeding there are now many colour varieties, including darker shades of green, blue, yellow, grey and olive.

Nomadic flocks

Budgerigars are gregarious and nomadic, travelling in large flocks. They have no fixed territories outside the breeding season. Instead they move from one feeding ground to another. Their voice is a churring warble interspersed at time with whistles and screams, and they readily mimic in captivity other sounds, including human speech.

Threat to grain crops

Originally its food was mainly grass seeds, but other seeds and fruits would be taken. With the spread of agriculture grain crops are attacked.

Life history

Breeding takes place in mallee scrub, which resembles silver birch, but the tree has several trunks springing from a common base. Where the stems meet, moisture is trapped and rotten wood results, and it is in these holes and crevices that budgerigars make their nests, chipping away to make holes 6 in. — 1 ft deep and about 2 in. wide.

430

In captivity it is not enough just to keep two budgerigars of the opposite sex together and expect them to breed. No matter how ardent the male's courtship, this alone is insufficient to stimulate egg-laying in his hen. The female needs a nest-box or total darkness for 24 hours each day and she must hear the male's loud and soft warbles. Eggs are laid on alternate days, incubation beginning as soon as the first egg has been laid. They hatch in a series after each egg has been incubated 18 days. A female blue hen is seen here with her chicks of varying ages.

H Lacev

▷ Overleaf: In the years after World War II the budgerigar became a very popular cage bird. The millions in captivity now probably exceed the hordes of wild ones that still inhabit Australia.

V Serventy: Photo Res.

△ The wild budgerigar is grass-green with yellow on the head and a long blue tail. Upper parts are barred and scalloped with black and yellow, with a royal blue patch on each cheek and three black spots on each side of the throat.

Graham Pizzey: NHPA

◁ Large flock of budgerigars swarming to drink in central Australia. They were imported into England by naturalist John Gould in 1840. Soon established in the aviaries of Europe they proved to be prolific breeders in captivity. From 1864 stocks began to produce colour variations differing from the natural green ones. Today, colours range from white to yellow or almost pink, from cobalt to green and grey.

▷ Overleaf: A flock of wild budgerigars on Nullarbor Plains, Western Australia.

Apart from chips of rotten wood and wood dust lying in the holes no nesting material is used.

Up to nine eggs are laid and there may be two broods a year. These are spherical, white, and are incubated for 18—20 days by the hen alone, who is fed by the male during this time. The young remain in the nest for 30—35 days, and are tended by the parents until fully fledged.

In captivity, budgerigars in an outside aviary can be allowed freedom from the cage during the breeding season. They will return to feed their young in the cage nest. Certain ones will fail to return but numbers remain fairly constant.

An egg for a song

Most people are content to suppose that if two birds of opposite sex are kept together in a cage or aviary they are likely, as a matter of course, to mate when the breeding season arrives. Those who keep birds are aware that this is a long way from the truth. Although it is true for canaries, pigeons, house sparrows and starlings, experiments have shown that in many species the proximity of a male, or even his ardent courtship, are insufficient to stimulate egg-laying in his hen. This is so with the budgerigar which needs a nest-box, or total darkness for 24 hours each day, which simulates the condition within the wild budgerigar nest. Unpaired hens, moreover, given suitable nest-boxes and allowed to hear the song of male budgerigars laid within 18 days, whereas those kept under the same conditions and not allowed to hear the voice of a male had failed to lay after a month.

The male budgie courts the female by such things as nudging her bill, bobbing his head to her and feeding her. He also 'talks' to her. By talking to her we mean making a number of different sounds. Prominent among these are a loud and a soft warble. The loud warble, it seems, influences the males. Budgerigars are sociable and the effect of the males making the loud warble is to bring themselves into breeding conditions. The soft warble, it now appears, causes the ovaries of the female to develop and the ova in them to ripen so that egg-laying may proceed. Moreover, this breeding condition is hastened when she can hear several males, even though she is in a cage, isolated with one male only.

Perhaps the most conclusive tests were those in which tape-recordings were used. A female with a nest-box and not exposed to long periods of light, or else kept in the dark, would lay on being allowed to hear a tape-recording of a male's soft warble. Further, if allowed to hear this for a total of 6 hours a day she was ready to lay in a shorter period of time than if presented with 'the voice' for 3 hours a day.

class	**Aves**
order	**Psittaciformes**
family	**Psittacidae**
genus & species	*Melopsittacus undulatus*

Bulbul

A family of 119 species of birds, related to the babblers. Some species vary over their geographical range while other species are difficult to tell apart, so classification is not easy, and some authors recognise fewer species.

The name is of Arab origin and is probably imitative. It is also Hindi and Persian for the white-cheeked bulbul. The nightingale in English translations of the Rubaiyat of Omar Khayyam *is actually this bulbul. It is an allowable emendation, as the white-cheeked bulbul has a song reminiscent of a nightingale.*

Bulbuls are small birds, ranging from the size of a house sparrow to that of a blackbird. The wings are short and the tail comparatively long, and several species fly only weakly. Around the base of the bill are well-developed bristles, which may help guide food into the mouth. A character not easily visible is a patch of hairlike feathers on the back of the neck. Some species have a distinct crest.

The plumage of the sexes is much the same, rarely very brilliant except in species with patches of yellow, red or white. African members of the genus Phyllastrephus *are often called brownbuls or greenbuls and have greenish or brownish backs and yellowish underparts. In these species the females are smaller than the males and have shorter bills.*

Gregarious songsters

Outside the breeding season, bulbuls are gregarious, living in noisy flocks, and sometimes mixing with other species. Many of them are good songsters. Most bulbuls are forest dwellers, but others live in sparse woodland or come into orchards and over various parts of the bulbuls' range certain species have established themselves as birds of garden and town, the equivalent of blackbirds or house sparrows in Europe. Bulbuls range the warmer parts of the Old World as shown on the map.

Tipsy bulbuls

Apart from the greenbuls that are mainly insect-eaters and have stouter bills, the bulbuls feed mainly on fruits and berries with some insects and spiders. Some drink nectar from flowers, and like other fruit-eating birds, bulbuls have been found in a tipsy state from eating overripe, fermenting fruit. The majority forage in the upper parts of trees, but the terrestrial bulbul of south eastern Africa searches for insects on the ground.

In a few places bulbuls are a pest, descending on fruit crops and stripping the trees bare. In the mountains of India the black bulbul attacks cherry orchards and small boys keep a non-stop guard to drive them off. They attach ropes to the top branches of the trees and stand in the middle, pulling the ropes to shake the tree whenever a bulbul lands.

TW Roth: Photo Res.

◁ Overleaf: Blackcrested yellow Bulbul, Pycnonotus flaviventris.

△ The African bulbul, P. barbatus, is widely distributed in Africa, with many races.

Elaborate courting ritual

The male courts the female by puffing out his body feathers to display the coloured patches that are often at the base of the tail. The female responds by chirping and quivering her wings. If she has a crest she retracts this.

The nest is cup-shaped and is built in a tree fork, usually near the ground. It is made of grass, pine needles, bamboo and other readily-available materials.

The hen lays 2 or 3 eggs, rarely 4 or 5, at one day intervals. Incubation then proceeds for 10–15 days, and is usually carried out by the female, who is fed by the male. Both parents feed the chicks.

Adults mob enemies

Mongooses, crows, magpies, owls and hawks often take the broods of bulbuls. The adults will, however, join together to mob these enemies.

Spreading suburbanite

Bulbuls are popular cage birds, especially in the Orient, as many are good songsters and are easy to tame. As they have been carried to different parts of the world, it is not surprising that some should have escaped from captivity, or been deliberately released. Different species of bulbuls have gone wild in Fiji, the West Indies, New Zealand, Australia and the United States. Wild populations of the red-whiskered bulbul have formed in Sydney, Melbourne and Florida, and of the red-vented in Fiji and Auckland. In Florida wild bulbuls were first seen in Kendall, just south of Miami. A few months later they had spread to Princeton, 35 miles away, and in 3 years the population numbered 40–50. Although in their natural habitat these birds are primarily forest-dwellers that became adapted to living in gardens, these immigrants stayed in the suburbs, not venturing out into the country. Perhaps they were able to get the right food from only suburban gardens.

The red-vented bulbuls appeared in Auckland in 1952 and in case they became pests, their further import was made illegal. At the same time much publicity was given to the birds, and the public were asked to report any they saw so movements could be recorded and steps taken to control them. Unfortunately the very process of making their import illegal probably encouraged the introduction of bulbuls, as captive birds were released on arrival at the ports, before the customs officers could find them.

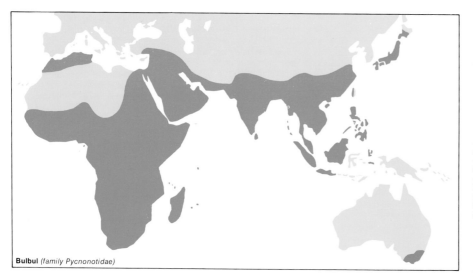

Bulbul (family Pycnonotidae)

class	**Aves**
order	**Passeriformes**
family	**Pycnonotidae**
genera & species	**Pycnonotus cafer** red-vented bulbul **P. jocosus** red-whiskered bulbul **P. leucogenys** white-cheeked bulbul **Hypsipetes madagascariensis** black bulbul others

BULLDOGS

The Bulldog is universally accepted as the national breed of Britain. Historians tell us that the Bulldog is one of the original and peculiar races of Britain—descended from those dogs of war that were so largely used by the Britons in their combats with the Romans. We have no certain proof of this but many believe that it is true. However, we do know that these same historians in writing of the Bulldog always stress its tenacity, courage and fighting spirit.

It is said that the sport of bull-baiting dates back to the time of King John. In the year 1209, William, Earl Warren was standing on the walls of his castle at Stamford in Lincolnshire watching two bulls fighting in the castle meadows. The fray brought the butchers' bull-dogs on the scene and they immediately attacked one of the bulls and chased it through the streets of the town. This so pleased the Earl he gave the meadows (after the first grass had been cut) to the butchers so that they could continue the sport for ever. Similar annual exhibitions were established at Tutbury, Staffordshire in 1374 and continued uninterrupted until the year 1778. The centre of Birmingham was also well known for holding these contests and the spot on which they took place is known today as the Bull Ring.

Tenacious

It was only by the untiring efforts of the clergy and by the eloquence of humane members of parliament that the abominable practice was stamped out. Abominable practice it certainly was, as much for the dogs as the bulls, for the owners of these dogs had a code all their own—the dog must attack in front, fastening on the lip, tongue or eye. It was then expected to hang on in spite of the most desperate efforts to dislodge it. Should a dog attack from behind it was looked upon as degenerate and was discarded as worthless. Puppies of six months were frequently tried against the bull to prove their mettle, but having acquitted themselves to the satisfaction of their owners they were not used until they attained the age of usefulness, usually about eighteen months. Many instances have been given over the years of the inhuman treatment these owners subjected the dogs to, to prove their courage.

Some years ago a certain Lancashire breeder was playing around with a litter of pups. Suddenly one of the pups grabbed his nose and held on. The breeder dashed from the kennel to the house crying to his son 'Be careful, don't pull him off or tha'll spoil him. Talk to him gentle and see if tha can get him to leggo.' The pain of his nose was not comparable to the pride of having bred a pup who knew his job.

From bull ring to show ring

Bull-baiting and bear-baiting was made illegal in 1835 and when the bill was passed prohibiting dog fighting there was a steady decline of interest in the breed. But certain men, such as the then Duke of Hamilton, kept a strain of pure-bred Bulldogs and it was due to the dedication of such men that the fighting dog was turned into the show dog. The first Bulldog is said to have been shown in 1860 by a Mr James Hinks in Birmingham and from then on the Bulldog was bred for exhibition and gradually regained its popularity. In 1875 the first Bulldog Club was formed. Its aim from the beginning had been to encourage purity of breed by fixing a definite Standard and maintaining reliable registers. The Club still flourishes today and still works for the same ideals.

The standard it set in those far-off days is still strictly adhered to by Bulldog Clubs all over the world. It has been said that no breed of dog has so elaborate a standard of points as the Bulldog and to a novice the many terms are often a matter of difficulty to comprehend.

The general appearance of the Bulldog is that of a smooth coated, thick-set dog, rather low in stature but broad, powerful and compact. The head is strikingly massive and large in proportion to the dog's size. The face is extremely short, the muzzle very broad, blunt and inclined upwards. The body is short and well knit, the limbs stout and muscular. The hindquarters are high and strong but rather lightly made in comparison with its fore-parts. The dog should convey an impression of determination, strength and activity, similar to that suggested by the appearance of a thick-set Ayrshire Bull.

The Bulldog is a unique British breed, with some very unusual characteristics, but its rather fearsome exterior hides a courageous and loyal nature.

Diane Pearce

435

Bullfinch

This is one of the most distinctive small birds that comes into an English garden. The rose-red underparts of the male, or the pinkish-grey of the female, when the bird is perched, are unmistakable. The back is grey and there is a black cap on the head. However, bullfinches are secretive and can most easily be identified by the pure white rump that is displayed in flight.

Bullfinches are extremely unpopular because of the damage they do by feeding on the buds of fruit trees. They can be a major pest of orchards, and recent work has shown how the amount of damage done is related to the size of the bullfinches' natural food supply.

Increasing numbers near man

Bullfinches are found across Europe and Asia from the British Isles to Japan. In most places they are restricted to coniferous or mixed woodlands, but in Japan and Britain they live in deciduous woodland and also come out into cultivated ground.

The British race of bullfinch is rather smaller and less brightly coloured than the European race which is only occasionally seen in the British Isles.

Since the 1940's bullfinches have increased in numbers in Britain, especially in the South of England. The increase cannot be fully explained, but the birds may have gained from having learnt to live near man. Apart from coming into farmland and parks to feed they will now nest near houses and the opening of new feeding and breeding grounds must have allowed a considerable increase in population.

Bullfinches are not often seen on the ground, where they hop rather heavily. Usually they perch in the cover of trees, flying with the typically finch-like undulating flight from one tree to another. Throughout most of the year they may be seen in pairs or small family parties. In the spring they may occasionally be seen in flocks, rarely of over 100 birds.

Bud-stripping pests in orchards

Bullfinches feed on buds and seeds, eating buds mainly in spring, those of fruit trees being preferred to the buds of woodland trees. A bullfinch feeds on buds systematically and efficiently landing on the tip of a branch and slowly moving in towards the trunk, stripping the buds as it goes. When it reaches the older wood where there are

Parent bullfinches at the nest with fledglings. The male is identified by his rosy-red underparts, the female by the pinkish-grey. The chicks are fed on a mixture of seeds and insects brought at first by the male to the female at the nest. The hen takes the food and feeds the chicks.

G. Rüppell

436

Jane Burton: Photo Res.

Fledgling that has just left the nest. Baby bullfinches learn their song from their father.

Ian Newton

Bullfinches do much damage to the buds of fruit trees. Here they have stripped the rows of their favourite variety, 'conference' pear blossom, and avoided the 'comice' variety on the right.

fewer buds it flies out to the tip of another branch. In this way it deals with up to 30 buds a minute. This is a very efficient method of removing buds and it is now common, especially in south-east England, for orchards capable of yielding several tons of fruit can be stripped by bullfinches so thoroughly that only a few pounds are harvested. However, this is an inefficient method of obtaining nutrition for the bullfinches as only the centres of the buds where the seeds eventually develop are eaten.

It is only when supplies of seeds, left over from the previous summer and autumn, are exhausted that bullfinches attack buds. Sometimes this may not occur until late spring, but when the last season's crop of seeds has been poor, buds may be taken throughout the winter.

In deciduous woods, the bullfinches show a very definite preference for the seeds of certain plants. These are docks, nettles, privet, bramble, birch and ash, with a very few seeds of other species. These seeds ripen in October forming a food supply that has to last until the buds develop. Birch and privet are preferred, but after all the others have been eaten, ash forms the bulk of the bullfinches' food supply. The size of the crop of ash seeds varies enormously with, typically, a two-year cycle of abundance. One year the crop is plentiful, the next very few seeds are produced. It is in these years of shortages that bullfinches turn to buds to make up their diet, and become such a pest in orchards.

Cock bullfinch—the breadwinner
Nests of fine twigs with moss and lichen and a lining of intertwined roots, always black, are built in shrubs and hedgerows, usually a few feet above the ground. There may be three clutches of 4–5 eggs laid in one season, from early May to mid-July, but if food is plentiful breeding may continue until October. The cock helps the hen incubate the eggs and also feeds her while she is on the nest. Chicks hatch out in a fortnight and are fed on a mixture of seeds and insects. At first the cock provides all the food, but later both parents collect food for the chicks, which fledge in just over a fortnight.

Half young killed by predators
Dr Ian Newton, studying bullfinches around Oxford, found that only $\frac{1}{3}$ of all clutches in woodland and $\frac{2}{3}$ of those in farmland were successful. The rest were eaten by predators, mainly jays which are more numerous in woodland, so accounting for the greater survival of young bullfinches in farmland. Magpies, stoats and weasels also prey on the broods.

The bullfinch has been persecuted in England since at least the 16th century and now that its numbers have been increasing, more efficient means of killing them are continually being sought. However, there is little sign of their numbers declining, for although large numbers may be shot or trapped in orchards, there is always a reserve breeding population in the woods waiting to replace them.

Birds as pests
As has already been stated, the bullfinches inflict the worst damage on orchards in years when there has been a poor crop of ash seed.

The reason for the ash trees all producing a good or a bad crop in a given year is itself interesting. The trees cannot get enough food to produce a good crop every year so they rest one year, building up supplies for the next. The years of abundance are synchronised because in a year of bad weather no trees will produce a good crop. Then the next year all will produce a good one. As the years pass, some trees get out of step, but another year of bad weather will bring them all back into line.

This enables bad bullfinch years to be predicted so it is possible to start trying to control them at the right time. Previously, fruit growers had started killing bullfinches as they moved into the orchards in spring. This was too late. Now trapping starts in the autumn, for, by removing a large part of the population early enough, the supplies of seeds will last longer and so delay the time when the bullfinches have to turn to buds.

When the bullfinches do turn to eating buds they eat some varieties of fruit before others. The buds of dessert apples are eaten before 'cookers' and striking contrasts may be seen in orchards where two varieties of fruit are grown in alternate rows. The one will be stripped, the other a mass of blossom. However, it is no good growing only the latter in the hope that a good crop will ensue. If their favoured varieties are absent they will not hesitate to eat others, although it has been shown with captive bullfinches that they thrive best on their preferred varieties.

class	**Aves**
order	**Passeriformes**
family	**Fringillidae**
genus & species	***Pyrrhula pyrrhula***

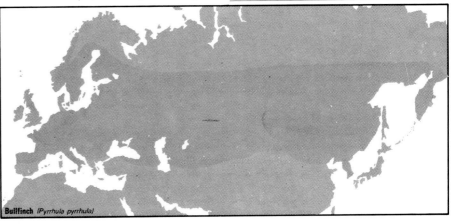
Bullfinch *(Pyrrhula pyrrhula)*

Bullfrog

The bullfrog is a large species of North American frog. The adults grow to be about 8 in. long. Its skin is usually smooth like that of a common frog but sometimes it is covered with small tubercles. The colour varies; on the upper parts it is usually greenish to black, sometimes with dark spots, the underparts are whitish with tinges of yellow. The females are browner and more spotted than the males. The best way of telling them apart is by comparing the size of the eye and the eardrum. In females they are equal, but in males the eardrum is larger than the eye.

The natural home of the bullfrog is in the United States, east of the Rockies, and on the northern borders of Mexico. They have also been introduced to the western states of America, as well as to Cuba, Hawaii, British Columbia, Canada.

The bullfrog's damp world

Bullfrogs are rarely found out of the water, except during very wet weather. They like to live near ponds and marshes or slow-flowing streams, lying idly along the water's edge under the shade of shrubs and reeds. In winter they hibernate, near the water, under logs and stones or in holes on the banks. How long they hibernate depends upon the climate. Usually they are the first amphibians in an area to retire and, in the spring, they are the last to emerge. In the northern parts of their range they usually emerge about the middle of May, but in Texas, for example, they may come out in February if the weather is mild enough. In the southern areas of their range they may not bother to hibernate at all.

A voracious appetite

The bullfrog gets most of its food from insects, earthworms, spiders, crayfish and snails. Many kinds of insects are caught including grasshoppers, beetles, flies, wasps and bees. The slow-moving larvae and immobile pupae, as well as the active adults, are taken. The unfortunate dragonfly is usually caught when it is in the middle of laying its eggs.

The bullfrog captures small, active prey like this by lying in wait and then leaping forward as the prey passes. Its tongue flies out by muscular contraction and wraps around the prey like a whiplash wrapping itself around a post. The frog then submerges to swallow its victim.

Its diet of insects, however, is usually supplemented by bigger prey. This can include other frogs and tadpoles and small terrapins and alligators. The bullfrog even eats snakes, including small garter and coral snakes. The fact that it eats these snakes is a measure of its voracity. Garter snakes themselves feed largely on amphibians and coral snakes are venomous. There is one case on record of a 17 in. coral snake being taken by a bullfrog. It can even capture small animals like mice and birds and especially ducklings. Even swallows, flying low over the water, are not safe from its voracious appetite and leaping ability.

Carl Mills

John Norris Wood

438

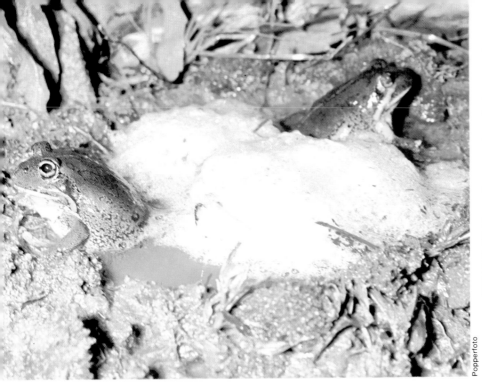

◁◁ *Bullfrog*, Rana catesbeiana. *It will take quite large prey including other frogs, small terrapins, and alligators, and even coral and garter snakes.*
◁ *Australian bullfrogs*, Limnodynastes dorsalis. *The female lays eggs in a mass of jelly which she beats up as the eggs are extruded so the eggs are coated and given protection.*
▽ *The bullfrog rarely leaves the water except during very wet weather. It lives in ponds, marshes or slow-flowing streams, and is often seen lying idly along the water's edge under the shade of reeds and shrubs.*

Popperfoto

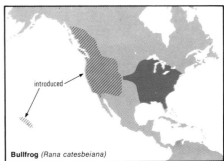

introduced

Bullfrog *(Rana catesbeiana)*

KB Newman

△ *African bullfrog*, Pyxicephalus adspersus, *can puff out its vocal sacs to bellow like a calf.*

Carl Mills

△ *With its powerful back legs, the bullfrog can leap over 3 ft. This ability helps in catching its prey; it lies in wait and leaps out on passing prey, catching it while it is in the air.*

Unusual mating call

When the water temperature reaches about 21°C/70°F mating takes place. This can be about February in the south of its range, to June or July in the northern parts. At night the males move out from the banks to call, while the females stay inshore. They join the male only when their eggs are ripe.

Find an empty barrel somewhere and shout into it, as deeply as possible, the word 'rum' and, according to Clifford Pope, the American herpetologist, the hollow, booming sound which will emerge is very like the mating call of the bullfrog. The call has also been described as sounding something like 'jug o' rum' or 'more rum' and the alcoholic allusion is carried a bit further in some parts by referring to the bullfrog as 'the jug o' rum'.

The bullfrog makes this extraordinary sound 3 or 4 times in a few seconds. Then, after an interval of about 5 minutes, it repeats it. The sound is made by air being passed back and forth along the bullfrog's windpipe, from lungs to mouth, with the nostrils closed. Some of the air enters the airsacs in the floor of the mouth and they swell out like balloons and act as resonators, amplifying the sound so that the noise can be heard ½ mile away.

After the mating the female bullfrog lays 10—25 thousand eggs which float in a sheet on the surface of the water, in among the water plants. With its envelope of jelly, each egg is just over ½ in. It is black above and white below. The eggs usually hatch within a week of being laid. If the temperature is low, however, they may take 2 years, sometimes more, to change into an adult frog, by which time they are 2—3 in. long. They feed on algae and decaying vegetation with occasional meals of small pond animals. After about another 2 years the young bullfrogs are almost fully grown and are ready to breed. One bullfrog at the London Zoo lived for 15½ years.

It's not easy to stay alive

Both the tadpole bullfrog and the adult have a lot of enemies. Fish, snakes, birds and mammals, such as skunks and racoons, all take their toll. A particular enemy of the tadpoles is the backswimmer, which grapples with a tadpole, inserts its 'beak' and sucks out the body fluids. All the bullfrog can do to protect itself from any enemy, apart from hiding at the bottom of the pool or stream, is to use its tremendous jumping powers to leap several feet clear.

Man is another enemy of the bullfrog. Men hunt them for their legs which are considered as much of a delicacy as those of the edible frog. In California, where they multiplied rapidly after their introduction half a century ago, limits had to be set on the numbers that could be collected in an attempt to prevent them being wiped out altogether. The usual method of killing them is to search for them after dark, dazzle them with a flashlight and then shoot before they can leap clear.

The jumping-frog that didn't jump

There are many ancient legends about 'jumping-frogs' and how their owners have been double-crossed. Mark Twain tells one of the best versions in a short story about one Jim Smiley of Angel's Camp, Calveras County, California. In the story Jim Smiley catches a frog. He calls it Dan'l Webster. The frog is a terrific jumper and Jim makes a lot of money betting on it in contests with other frogs. Then a stranger arrives in the camp and says that he does not think that Dan'l, the frog, is that good a jumper. He's quite prepared to back his word with 40 dollars. The trouble is that, being a stranger, he does not have a frog. Unwilling to let 40 dollars slip by so easily Jim Smiley goes off to find a frog. He leaves his frog with the stranger.

Eventually the new frog is lined up alongside Dan'l Webster. The starting signal is given and both frogs are prodded. The new frog leaps away. Dan'l Webster doesn't move an inch. The stranger collects his 40 dollars and smugly takes his leave. Jim Smiley is baffled and furious.

He can't imagine what's happened to his champion frog. Maybe it's ill. So he picks it up to have a look.

'Why, bless my oats,' he exclaims, 'if he don't weigh a double handful of shot!' So he turns Dan'l Webster, the champion frog, upside down and out pours a couple of pounds of lead shot.

Mark Twain's story was a roaring success. In 1928 when a celebration was held in Angel's Camp, to mark the paving of the streets, the ceremonies included, naturally, a frog-jumping contest. The winner was an entrant called 'Jumping Frog of the San Joaquin' with a leap of 3 ft 4 in.

The contest became very popular and it is now held every year. Allowances are even made for the unpredictable natures of the frogs. Because the first jump might be short and the second record-breaking the contest is judged on the distance travelled by the frog in three consecutive leaps. The record now stands at over 16 ft. So many entries are attracted every year that a stringent set of rules is enforced. One can surely presume that all entries are weighed before jumping so that competitors are spared the embarrassing experience of Jim Smiley—whose tortured ghost is said still to haunt the arena.

class	**Amphibia**
order	**Salientia**
family	**Ranidae**
genus & species	*Rana catesbeiana* *bullfrog*

Bullhead

This fish was first called 'miller's thumb', after the broad splayed shape of the end of a miller's thumb, caused by constantly rubbing flour between thumb and fingers to gauge its texture. Since at least 1450, however, it has been known as the bullhead. Several different kinds of fishes have been called this name but priority must be given to the freshwater fish of European rivers Cottus gobio. It belongs to the family Cottidae, and most species in this family are marine fishes.

The bullhead is 3−4 in., rarely up to 6 in. long, with a broad, flattened head rounded in front, and a stout body tapering to the tail. Its fins are large and spiny and there is a stout spine on the gill-cover. The colour is variable, greenish-yellow to brown with dark bars and blotches, and it changes with the emotions of fear or aggression, and also to harmonize with its background when it is resting on a stony bed.

Bullhead relatives in North America are called sculpins, and the catfishes there are called bullheads. The catfishes of the family Ameiuridae found in North and middle America are also called bullheads. They are more or less tadpole-shaped, with a large, broad head and a strongly compressed tail region.

A marine fish of the family Sciaenidae is also known in the southern United States as a bullhead. In New Zealand a small goby has been called a bullhead.

Bullhead bullies

The bullhead is solitary in the shallows in clear, gently-flowing streams or in lakes, lurking on the gravel or beneath stones, moving little except to feed or when disturbed. Then it darts rapidly away, at such a speed that the eye can only just follow it. This, then, is the function of its fine set of fins, to give it manoeuvrability among the stones on the bed of the stream or lake, but it cannot swim any great distance. Hunting bullheads has been a popular juvenile sport for centuries but they must be approached with care since they are highly aggressive fish. To put a finger into the entrance to its retreat is to risk having the fish nip it. A fish of either sex with its home under a stone will drive off a smaller fish that looks in, merely by using an aggressive display. If a larger bullhead looks in, the smaller occupant swims out, yielding its territory.

Attacks larger fishes

Feeding is mainly, if not wholly, at night. Its usual food is insects, their larvae, freshwater shrimps and fry, but it will take almost any animal food coming its way that it can swallow. It will also attack other fishes as large or larger than itself. It usually attacks only food that swims, rarely touching anything that crawls over, or lies on, the bottom. It has been accused of depredations on salmon eggs but the few it takes are probably those being laid.

A bullhead takes $3-3\frac{1}{2}$ days to digest its smaller prey, 5−6 days to digest a meal of fish, the bones softening towards the end of this time.

Bullhead, Cottus gobio, resting on a stony stream bed. When it is still, it will change its colour to harmonize with the background as seen here. This 3−4in. freshwater European fish will also change colour with the emotions of fear or aggression when danger threatens.

Robin Fletcher

JM Clayton: NHPA

△ *The spines on the breast fins and gill-covers give protection from all but the larger fishes.*

▽ *The bullhead probably has few predators. This one is being eaten by a Slavonian grebe.*

Jane Burton: Photo Res.

Gill-cover spines give protection

The spines on its gill-covers and in its fins must give protection from all but the larger predatory fishes. Herons will take bullheads and owls are reported to do so, but there have been reports of water birds, such as grebe, having been found dead, choked in their attempts to swallow a bullhead. On the whole, it is probably true to say there are no serious predators.

It used to be said that the bullhead makes curious sounds due to terror when captured. The modern view is that it uses a part of the gill-cover for stridulation, but whether as a sign of fear or as a warning has not yet been proved.

Late leavers eaten by father

Spawning is in March to April. The male scoops a hollow in sand under a stone, his female then laying her orange-coloured egg-mass, of up to 250 eggs, usually on the ceiling of the nest-shelter. These take 1 month to hatch, during which time they are guarded by the male, who also aerates them by fanning with his pectoral fins. Unless the nests are in running water, the eggs soon become attacked by fungus if the male is killed or taken away. The fry do not leave the nest for a while, and are guarded until they leave and disperse. Any that remain in the nest, probably the more weakly ones, are eaten by the male parent.

Bullhead's ostrich habit

Many a youngster, hunting bullheads, must have noticed how the fish will dive under stones and be quite content provided its head is under cover. Its waving tail is still exposed, and if this is gently and firmly grasped, the fish can be held and lifted out of the water. The cause of this ostrich-like behaviour is twofold. A bullhead has the impulse to move away from the light, as assuredly as a green plant moves towards it. This is not unusual in nocturnal animals and, indeed, partly explains why they are nocturnal. A bullhead is uncomfortable except when in the dark or semi-dark. In fact, if the sky is heavily overcast it will come out to feed, as if night were falling. The second thing is that the bullhead is comfortable by day only if it can feel some part of its body, if only a fin, pressing against a solid support. So, with its head in darkness and one or more of its fins pressed against a stone, it gets a sense of security even though ¾ of its body is exposed.

This, naturally, is a dangerous situation for the bullhead, so far as natural enemies are concerned. It explains, among other things, why a grebe should be choked, because it does not have the trick of a true fish-eater, of turning the fish in its beak to swallow it headfirst.

class	**Osteichthyes**
order	**Scorpaeniformes**
family	**Cottidae**
genus & species	***Cottus gobio***

Bumble-bee covered with pollen. Flying from one flower to another the bumble-bee transfers the pollen from one flower to a similar type and so cross-fertilisation results.
John Markham

Bumble-bee

Bumble-bees are rather like honey-bees except that they have a larger body which is covered with stiff yellow, orange or red hairs. The bumble-bee also has a sting which it can use to inject venom into the body of an enemy. The sting is a modified ovipositor—a tube-like organ used by other insects to deposit their eggs.

Bumble-bees are also known as 'humble-bees'. Both names come from the lazy humming sound made by the bee as it flies from one flower to another.

The bumble-bee is found all over the world. Most species live in the tropical or sub-tropical zones but they can also be found in places as far apart as Arctic Canada and Tierra del Fuego, and the equivalent of this range in the Old World. They are not native to Australasia, but were introduced there when settlers found that none of the local bees would pollinate the red clover plant which they had introduced. So the bumble-bee was brought in to do the job.

Buzzing around from flower to flower

Under a microscope the hindleg of a bumble-bee is an interesting sight. The outer face of the 'shin' is flat and polished but along each side there is a row of stiff bristles. These bristles make up what is called the pollen basket. If you watch a bumble-bee flying from one flower to another it is quite easy to see the large yellow balls of pollen attached to its hindlegs. When the bee forces its way into a flower the pollen is rubbed off onto its body hairs. The bee then brushes the pollen from its body, moistens it with a little nectar and sticks it onto the pollen basket. When it gets back to the nest it uses its forelegs to remove the balls of pollen from this basket and put them into the egg-cell.

The bumble-bee is attracted to the flower by the nectar, which it sucks up through a special extendible tube. The nectar is then stored away in the crop or honey stomach.

Flowers and bees depend upon each other for their existence. The bee benefits from the pollen and the flowers benefit by being 'cross-pollinated'. This cross-pollination occurs when some of the pollen from one flower is rubbed off onto another flower, thus fertilising it.

It is for this reason, to attract bees rather than people, that flowers have evolved their attractive colours and scents.

Rise and fall of a queen bee

Usually it is a pure accident if an insect meets one of her offspring. This is because most insects lay their eggs and then leave them to hatch out by themselves.

Some insects, however, are different. They are called social insects. This kind of insect stays with her offspring and they, in turn, stay with her and help look after her next brood. Wasps, honey-bees and ants are all well-known examples of social insects. In their case thousands of individuals live in one nest. Most of them are sexless or, rather, under-developed females. These workers care for the breeding female, the queen, and for her eggs and larvae. Bumble-bees are social insects too, but their communal life is not as well developed as the others. There are fewer workers in the colony and they all die before the winter.

The life of a bumble-bee colony begins in autumn. A young female bumble-bee leaves the nest, mates and finds a sheltered spot where she can spend the winter hibernating. When spring comes—the actual date depends upon the species—the young queen emerges and suns herself until she is fully active. Then off she flies in search of pollen and nectar from the spring flowers. The queen needs pollen because it contains large amounts of protein which is used to build up in her ovaries the eggs to be laid later.

Soon the queen starts looking for a suitable place to build her nest. She might take over the abandoned nest of a fieldmouse, a vole, or a hedgehog. Or she might pick somewhere else: a disused bird's nest, a thatched roof, a bale of hay or even a discarded mattress. Her favourite sites are along hedgerows and banks or in old, neglected corners of fields and gardens. Nowadays it is not easy for the queen bee to find this kind of place. Modern intensive and mechanised farming demands that these unproductive corners be ploughed up so that every square foot of ground pays its way. The result is that bumble-bees, which are in a sense vital to the pollination of crops, are themselves becoming scarcer.

The queen usually builds her nest at the end of a tunnel. The tunnel may be several feet long, if she has used an old mouse nest, but some species prefer tunnels only a few inches long, so they build their nests in thatch or similar places. Some kinds of bumble-bees, known as carder-bees, even manage to build their nests on the surface. They do this by combing grass and other material into a tight, closely-woven ball.

If the queen has taken over the nest from a former occupant there is always plenty of nest material readily available. She fashions this into a small inner chamber lined with only the finest grass and roots. She stays in here for a day or two drying it out with her body heat. Insects are cold-blooded, but the larger ones generate enough heat, especially with their flight muscles, to keep their bodies a few degrees above air temperature outside the nest.

Food in a 'honey pot'

By now the eggs are developing inside the queen bee. She begins to make an egg-cell out of wax. The wax is secreted from between the plates on the underside of her abdomen. She goes out to collect pollen which she stores in the egg-cell, in which 8—14 eggs are laid. The cell is then covered

Male mating with queen bee Bombus ogrorum. *Young males are produced at the end of the season. After mating the queen finds a sheltered spot where she can spend the winter hibernating until the spring.*

Bumble-bee queen, B. hortorum, *incubating her first batch of brood which have reached the pupal stage. She stores surplus nectar in a wax 'honey pot' near the entrance of the nest to provide food in bad weather.*

with a cap of wax. The queen spends some of her time settled on top of the eggs to keep them warm. She also goes out feeding and brings home any surplus nectar which she stores in a 'honey pot' near the entrance to the nest. The 'honey pot' is made of wax and is about ¾ in. high and ½ in. across. It provides a source of food when the weather is too bad for the queen to go out foraging.

When the larvae begin to hatch out of the eggs they are just helpless maggots with very little in the way of legs or sense organs. They do nothing except feed on the pollen which has been stored in the egg-cell and on the mixture of nectar and pollen which their mother regurgitates to them. But they grow amazingly quickly on this diet. They shed their skins several times and then spin a cocoon and pupate.

At this point the queen carefully removes the wax from around the cocoons and makes it into new egg-cells. She puts these on top of the cocoons and lays the next batch of eggs in them. Eventually the first brood emerge from their cocoons as fully developed workers. They spend a day or two drying out while their wings expand and harden. Then they are ready to go out collecting food and to tend the next batch of larvae.

Before long a whole colony of several hundred workers has been built up. The queen, however, never becomes a helpless egg-laying machine as happens with ants and termites. She can still make egg-cells and feed larvae although she hardly ever leaves the nest to forage.

Towards the end of the summer, some of the eggs produce males and fertile females. The males develop by parthenogenesis — that is to say, from unfertilised eggs. The females, the next generation of queens, appear at first to be exactly the same as the sterile female workers but they grow much larger and eventually leave the nest to mate with the males. The males differ from other bumble-bees by having larger antennae,

which they use to locate the females. They do not have a sting.

Once the old queen has produced the males and the new queens she stops laying worker eggs. Gradually the whole colony dies out. After mating the males also die. It is winter again and only the young queens are left to survive through to spring.

Bumble-bees fighting for their lives

Bumble-bees have many enemies, large and small. The worst ones are insect-eating birds like the bee-eater, but there are plenty of others. Badgers or skunks and other mammals will dig up bees' nests both for the honey and for the bees themselves.

Naturalists once observed a skunk scratching at a nest until the irate inhabitants flew out. The skunk caught each one in its forepaws and killed it by rubbing it against the ground.

Fieldmice and shrews also attack bumble-bee nests, and among the smaller animals that are enemies of the bees are robber flies. They grapple the bees with their legs and suck their blood. Then there are the 'mites' which live in the air-sacs or 'lungs' of the bees and also suck their juices. Another enemy is the wax moth. It lays its eggs in bumble-bee nests and its caterpillars ruin the egg-cells by burrowing through them.

The cuckoo-bee is a close relative of the bumble-bee and in its own way another enemy. Cuckoo-bees do not have pollen baskets with which to collect stores of pollen. So instead they invade the nests of bumble-bees and lay their eggs there. The eggs develop into males and females, but not workers, and they have to be tended by the bumble-bee workers.

In a fight the bumble-bee will defend itself by biting and stinging. It rolls onto its back, with its jaws open and sting protruding, and sometimes squirts venom into the air. Its sting is not barbed, like the sting of a honey bee, so it can be withdrawn from the corpse of an enemy and used again.

More old-maids to strengthen the pound?

Charles Darwin began many controversies with his famous book *On the Origin of Species*. One of the things he mentioned in the book was that only bumble-bees visit the flowers of the red clover. This is because the red clover has a long, narrow flower and other bees do not have long enough tongues to reach the nectar which lies at the base of the flowers.

Darwin pointed out that if bumble-bees became rare or extinct the red clover would also die out. This would have serious economic effects, he said, because cattle are fed on red clover.

He went on to quote a Mr H Newman who said that more than two-thirds of bumble-bee nests in England are destroyed by mice. He claimed that bumble-bee nests were more common near villages and towns, where cats were plentiful. Therefore a large number of cats would mean a larger crop of clover because the cats would eat the mice who killed the bees.

Later a German scientist intervened to remark that a large number of cats would be good for England's economy because he considered England's wealth to be based on her cattle.

In a true Darwinian spirit, TH Huxley then stepped in to supply the final link. He suggested that, since old-maids were very fond of cats, the sensible way to strengthen the economy of the country would be to increase the number of old-maids. Less weddings and more spinsters was the short answer, according to Huxley.

class	**Insecta**
order	**Hymenoptera**
family	**Bombidae**
genus	***Bombus***

A batch of cocoons, two of which have been cut open to show the pupae inside. These will emerge as fully developed workers and will then spend a day or two drying out while their wings expand and harden (8 × lifesize).

When the temperature of their nests becomes too high some of the workers fan currents of air with their wings to cool the nests (B. ogrorum).

445

△ *The bumble-bee sucks up a large quantity of nectar through its proboscis so it has enough fuel in its honey tank in the body to return to the nest.*

▽ *The bee then builds up two bulging loads of pollen in the 'baskets' on the hindlegs. The bee seen here has its baskets bulging with a pollen load.*

Bunting

The best-known bunting in the British Isles is the yellowhammer, or yellow bunting. Even those who have not noticed its yellow head and underparts and chestnut, black-streaked upper parts will probably be familiar with its 'little bit of bread and no cheese' song, with the 'cheese' drawn-out and high-pitched.

Also common, but easily overlooked, are the reed buntings, the males of which have a dark head and 'bib' similar to those of the cock house sparrow. The female buntings are usually inconspicuous dull brown birds, and it is difficult to distinguish the hens of different species.

In the Old World, the name 'bunting' is used for members of the subfamily Emberizinae. The North American members of this subfamily are usually known as 'sparrows' or 'finches'. In America, 'bunting' is usually reserved for the colourful members of a very closely related subfamily that includes cardinals.

Old World buntings are finch-like birds with short, conical beaks used for crushing seeds, but of a slighter build and longer tail than the American 'buntings'. Their flight is, however, rather like that of sparrows or finches.

Flies in the far north

Buntings are widely distributed over Europe, Asia and Africa, most of them preferring open country, such as bush or grasslands. A few live in open woods or on the fringes of forests, but they are not often found in the denser forests. The breeding grounds of the snow bunting, with its conspicuous white head, breast and rump, range from the highlands of Scotland to the northern tip of Greenland, and in equivalent latitudes all round the Arctic, farther north than any other land bird.

Many buntings are migratory, moving south in the autumn and returning to the breeding grounds in spring. Of the 17 species recorded in the British Isles only 5 have bred. The others are migrants on passage, such as the ortolan bunting that is seen, mainly along the east and south coasts of England, in autumn and spring. These visitors are usually on their way to or from their breeding grounds in continental Europe but have been blown off course across the North Sea or the English Channel.

Outside the breeding season many buntings form flocks, often joining with finches and other species of bunting, both for feeding and roosting. The inconspicuousness of some species of bunting is heightened by their wariness. The ortolan bunting of northern and eastern Europe and the eastern Mediterranean is a very dull little bird with secretive habits, but the snow bunting and house bunting show little fear of man, and even nest in houses.

Ortolan eats locusts

Buntings feed on the seeds of plants, especially grasses, and on invertebrate animals, such as flying insects and their larvae, as well as snails and crustaceans. The relative amounts of the different foods vary with the species and the season. The ortolan bunting feeds on locusts during its migrations across Africa.

Eskimo winter for snow bunting

The arrival of snow buntings at their breeding ground and the establishment of their territory are described clearly in Niko Tinbergen's book *Curious Naturalists*. Having spent a winter amongst the Eskimos of East Greenland, Tinbergen could watch the snow buntings from the moment they arrived, a time of excitement for the Eskimos, as this heralded the coming of spring. The males turn up first to spend their time feeding and roosting. Later they start 'arguing' among themselves over the boundaries of the territories. The snow buntings sing from lookout points on boulders or fly into the air while singing to inform other snow buntings of their territory. If any strange bird wanders into the territory the owner will chase it out, and when two neighbours meet at the boundary, they indulge in a strange 'pendulum flight'. Each bird alternately advances and retreats so that the two birds fly backwards and forwards over the boundary as if linked by an invisible rod.

Eventually the females arrive and courtship begins. A notable feature of the courtship of buntings is the 'sexual chase', in which the male rushes after the female, chasing her in a headlong, twisting and turning pursuit until he catches her, whereupon a fluttering and tumbling brawl develops, both birds falling to the ground.

The nest is usually cup-shaped, or domed in the tropical species, and is made, often only by the female, out of grass, fine roots, moss and lichens. Most species nest a few feet off the ground. The reed bunting often builds its nest in reeds or sedges over water, others build their nests in tree-holes, while the rock, snow and Lapland buntings nest on the ground amongst rocks and hummocks.

The eggs number 2–6 and are incubated for 12–13 days. In some species both sexes

The reed bunting, Emberiza schoeniclus. *The easiest way of recognising this bunting is by its wide white collar.*

share incubation and feeding of the young; in others, this is left to the female.

Bigamy has been recorded in the corn bunting: 15 cock buntings in Cornwall were found to be siring 51 hens between them, some cocks having as many as 7 hens. The males, quite understandably, did not help rear the families. They spent their time on the look-out for intruders, while their hens built nests and raised chicks, often within a few yards of each other.

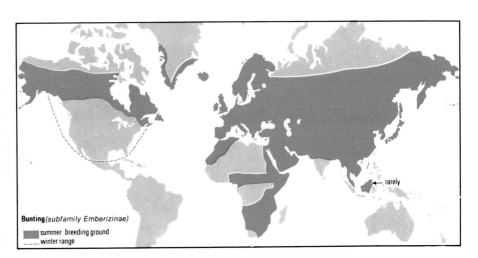

Bunting *(subfamily Emberizinae)*
■ summer breeding ground
--- winter range

← rarely

Territory turmoil

In 1920 an amateur ornithologist published a book that opened up new horizons in biological research and thought. The book was *Territory in Bird Life*, written by Eliot Howard, who made special studies of reed buntings and yellowhammers, as well as other birds that lived around his home. In the book he put forward the theory of territory, suggesting that the aggressiveness and song of male birds served to space the pairs out so that each had enough room to feed and bring up their young.

The idea of birds spacing themselves out like this was not new. The 17th-century biologist Ray wrote, 'It is proper to this bird at its first coming to occupy and seize upon one place as its freehold, into which it will not admit any other nightingale but its mate.' This is a clear statement that nightingales hold territories, and a hundred years later Gilbert White wrote, 'During the amorous season, such a jealousy prevails between the male birds that they can hardly bear to be together in the same hedge or field.' Later he said, 'It is to this spirit of jealousy that I chiefly attribute the equal dispersion of birds in spring over the face of the country.'

During the 19th century these ideas were forgotten, as ornithologists became more interested in collecting dead birds for studies of distribution and classification. It was the publication of Eliot Howard's book describing how flocks of yellowhammers broke up in the spring and the males became isolated, singing from favourite perches while keeping watch for intruders, that stimulated ornithologists to investigate the behaviour of other species. With few exceptions, their observations were the same — birds were spacing themselves out in territories, whether they were of several acres for a blackbird or a couple of square feet for an Adélie penguin (see p. 19). Ideas were put forward as to the mechanism of the spacing and its value to the birds, and further studies showed that territorial behaviour was not confined to birds. Animals as widely separated as dogs and fiddler crabs have special patterns of behaviour that result in their populations being spaced out. It is now suggested that much of human conflict, from wars between nations to brawls in the street, is due to this same basic concept of territory, although in human terms the territory need not mean an expanse of ground. Among scientists, for example, it can mean a field of study, and often there has been bickering or even bad blood between scientists because one has resented another 'intruding into his territory', as represented by a particular field of study.

class	**Aves**
order	**Passeriformes**
family	**Emberizidae**
subfamily	**Emberizinae**
genera	**Emberiza** ortolan, yellowhammer +35 species **Melophus** crested buntings **Plectrophenax** snow bunting **Calcarius** Lapland bunting or longspur, others

△ *Snow bunting*, Plectrophenax nivalis, *feeding young. They are circumpolar in the far north.*

▽ *Yellowhammer*, Emberiza citrinella. *It is found in Europe and Asia west of the Yenisei River.*

Burnet moth

The bright colours of the burnet moths make them very conspicuous. They are small with thick bodies, long forewings and short hindwings; the antennae are thickened near the tip and then pointed. Most are brightly coloured, the forewings dark metallic blue or green with scarlet markings and usually separate spots, the hindwings with a black border. This applies to all the British species, but in southern Europe white and yellow-spotted ones occur. In the beautiful Zygaena carniolica, of central and southern Europe and western Asia, the red spots are surrounded by white rings. Occasionally yellow-spotted forms occur in Britain as rare varieties of the normally red-spotted species.

Burnets from around the coasts of the Mediterranean occur in immense numbers and great variety. They extend in small numbers to temperate Asia and southern Africa and also into northern Europe, seven species being found in the British Isles. They belong to the family Zygaenidae which has many species with very metallic-looking colours and often bizarre-shaped wings. One subfamily of Zygaenidae has species where the hind wing, instead of the normal rather rounded shape, is thin and forms long trailing streamers behind the forewings.

Many of the brightly coloured species are day fliers, their colours warning predators that they are distasteful. In Europe some of the species are of very local distribution and many are confined to limestone districts where the soil is suitable for their food-plants to grow.

Moths in a meadow

Burnets usually live in colonies, often occupying only part of a hillside or a single meadow, and the colonies may persist for a few years and then die out. In a flourishing colony, the moths are often abundant, sometimes half-a-dozen or more being seen on a single flower-head.

The burnets are all day-flying moths and are most active when the sun is shining. The flight is slow and buzzing, and when at rest the moths are sluggish and can easily be captured without a butterfly net.

Tubular tongues for nectar

The adult moths feed on the nectar of flowers, sitting on the flower-heads and probing the nectaries with their long tubular tongues. The caterpillars feed on the leaves of low-growing plants. The food-plants of the three common British species are trefoils and clover. The mountain burnet feeds on crowberry, and one of the other northern species on thyme.

Annual life cycle

Normally the burnets have an annual life cycle, the caterpillars feeding during the late summer, hibernating through the winter and completing their growth during the

GE Hyde

△ *Burnet moth,* Zygaena trigonellae, *drying its wings (5 × lifesize).*

▽ *The beautiful* Zygaena carniolica *is found in central and southern Europe and western Asia.*

Yves Lanceau

449

Turquoise burnet moth, Procris statices.

spring and early summer of the following year. The mountain burnet is exceptional in taking more than one and possibly as much as four years to complete its life-cycle. Only a short time is spent as a pupa and the adult moths probably live only two or three weeks.

The caterpillars are thick and slug-shaped, green or yellow with a regular pattern of black spots. The pupa is enclosed in a characteristic spindle-like cocoon of parchment-like silk, shining yellow or white in colour. The cocoons are usually attached to a stem of grass or some other plant, those of the commoner species being conspicuous and easy to find. After the moth has hatched the black empty pupa shell always sticks out of the cocoon.

Safety in nastiness

Their habits would seem to make the burnets an easy prey for birds and other insect-eating animals, since they are slow-flying, conspicuous, and make no attempt to hide, and little to evade capture. They are all very ill-tasting, however, and to some degree poisonous, so that a bird which has pecked one of them is never likely to attack another. Their conspicuous appearance is associated with this, as it is to their advantage to be easily recognisable so that predators have no difficulty in learning to avoid them. Another day-flying moth, the cinnabar *Callimorpha jacobaeae*, of Europe and western

Burnet moth caterpillar, magnified 8 times, feeding on trefoil, one of its food-plants.

but not for long.

Within seconds it was almost literally running round in circles, stopping every so often to bite at cool grass blades or to rub its beak on the grass, the bare earth, or any stick or stone it came across, while saliva dripped from its beak. From time to time it spread its wings in the manner that has come to be associated with birds that have something acrid or pungent in the mouth.

Clearly the rook was agitated and going through an unpleasant experience, one it was unlikely to forget. The bill-cleaning and

agitated movement went on for some minutes. Moreover, during that time it repeatedly attacked its companion, with whom it had just been feeding harmoniously, chasing it with vicious stabs of the beak.

phylum	**Arthropoda**
class	**Insecta**
order	**Lepidoptera**
family	**Zygaenidae**
genus	*Zygaena*

Six-spot burnet, the commonest British species.

Five-spot burnet moths mating on an empty cocoon that has an empty pupa shell sticking out of it.

Asia, quite unrelated to the burnets, has a similar red and black pattern and is also protected by having a nasty taste.

The poison of the burnet moths is discharged in the form of a yellow fluid from the region of the neck, and it contains, among other substances, histamine and prussic acid (hydrogen cyanide).

In bad taste

A rook living in an aviary with a magpie as a companion was offered a burnet moth, experimentally, to see whether it would accept or reject it. It picked up the moth, dismembered it in rook fashion, by severing the wings and biting off the head. Then it took the body of the moth into its mouth—

451

Burrowing owl

The burrowing owl stands only 9 in. high, about the same size as the little owl of Europe and Asia. It is much the same colour as a little or a tawny owl but has a very short tail and long legs. The habit of bobbing up and down when on a perch is very characteristic of the species.

Threatened by farmers

The burrowing owl was once common on the plains and prairies of America, but the encroachment of agriculture has greatly restricted its range. Apart from ploughing ruining their burrows, these owls were shot because of the chance that horses or cattle might break legs in their holes. Families of burrowing owls have also been killed indiscriminately by poison gas used against ground squirrels. Providing that the terrain is not altered too much, however, burrowing owls should be able to hold their own, as farmers are now realizing that these and other owls are mainly beneficial because of the mice and insects they eat.

The burrowing owl ranges from the Pacific coast of America east to Minnesota and Louisiana. It breeds as far north as British Columbia and Manitoba and south to Tierra del Fuego, but does not occur in the forests of the Amazon basin. To the east it is found in Florida and on some of the West Indian islands, including the Bahamas, Haiti and the Lesser Antilles. In winter, some burrowing owls migrate from the northern parts of the range and the Florida population disappears outside the breeding season.

Hunts under sun or moon

Hunting takes place at any time of the day or night. The owls pounce on the prey, burying their talons into the victim's back, and peck viciously at its neck. Mice and small rats such as sage rats, ground squirrels and young cottontail rabbits, chipmunks and even bats are eaten. Insects are a large item of the diet, especially large beetles and grasshoppers, which are caught in the air with the talons. Very few birds are eaten, except during the breeding season when large numbers of newly-fledged birds, especially larks, are taken.

Other animals are included in the diet as the remains of scorpions and centipedes are sometimes found near burrows, and crayfish are commonly eaten by burrowing owls living near water. Whether the owls enter the water to catch them is not known; they may simply take advantage of crayfishes cast up on the banks or left exposed by a drought.

Burrowing owls have also been reported to eat members of their own kind but often this cannibalism has been shown to be the result of a burrowing owl finding a carcase rather than killing a fellow owl.

Like the little owl, the burrowing owl is more diurnal in its habits than most owls. The outcome of some experiments on the keenness of sight in owls showed that whereas barn owls and long-eared owls could find dead mice in light intensities equivalent to one candle nearly 2 000 ft away, burrowing owls were hard put to locate prey in light intensities far greater. Their sensitivity to light is in fact about the same as ours.

Young hiss like a snake

The eggs and chicks of burrowing owls are especially vulnerable to predators. Skunks, opossums and snakes, and probably domestic cats, destroy the nests of burrowing owls, unless the owners can drive them away. In the West Indies, introduced mongooses have wiped out the burrowing owls in Antigua, Nevis, St Kitts and Marie Galante.

When disturbed in the burrow, the young

△ *Burrowing owls preening. These 9 in. birds pounce on prey, and viciously peck the neck.*
◁ *Burrowing owl at entrance to its burrow.*

National Film Board, Canada

Zool. Soc. Lond.

Burrowing owl *(Speotyto cunicularia)*

get a certain measure of safety by their rattling hiss, remarkably like that of an irate rattlesnake.

Empty burrows taken over

As their name implies, burrowing owls make their nests in holes in the ground rather than in trees. They dig holes by scraping with their talons, but also take advantage of holes made by a wide variety of other animals. The holes of prairie dogs, woodchucks, American badgers, tortoises, armadillos, foxes, skunks and many others are taken over, and enlarged if necessary. The nesting chamber, lined with grass, feathers and other materials, is usually made at the end of a tunnel 5 ft or more long. The tunnel is about 5 in. wide and often has a sharp bend in it.

Both parents incubate the eggs, which number 6–11, for a month. The young leave the nest before they can fly and roost near the entrance, rushing forward whenever a parent arrives with food. When not hunting, the parents stand guard on a favourite perch, their 'cack-cack-cack-cack' alarm call sending the chicks running back into the nest at times of danger. This call, together with the cooing notes used in courting, has led the burrowing owl to be nicknamed the 'cuckoo-bird' in the West Indies and South America.

Burrowing owls used to breed in colonies but since the end of the last century these have largely disappeared and it is only in suitable terrain where there is abundant food that ten or more pairs may have burrows within 2–3 acres of ground.

Not the best of neighbours

There are often sections in popular books on animals dealing with animal partnerships in which examples are given of animals living together, usually to the benefit of both partners. An example often given is of burrowing owls sharing holes with viscachas, ground squirrels, or snakes such as rattlesnakes or hognosed snakes. It is then suggested that this 'happy family' live together to their mutual benefit. The burrowing owls, it is said, act as sentries, uttering their alarm calls when danger threatens, the snakes deter or kill any enemy and, we presume, the ground squirrels or other rodents provide company or warmth, or perhaps merely attract these useful tenants, the owls and snakes, by digging suitable burrows. These stories may be accompanied by a picture of owls, snakes and rodents all together in one large nest.

Nothing could be less likely. This is one of many stories, repeated again and again, with no observations to support them. At least a century ago, it was pointed out that burrowing owls move into burrows after the rodent owners have moved out. What is more, the owls prey on the rodents, especially the young ones. The behaviour of the snakes is even more at variance with the popular story. They seek any hole or crevice to hide in, but they do not hesitate to eat the broods of any birds or mammals they find there.

Another feature of this association that is unfavourable to the ground squirrels is that the burrowing owls become infested with their fleas, so carrying them from one squirrel colony to another, and these fleas carry plague germs.

class	**Aves**
order	**Strigiformes**
family	**Strigidae**
genus & species	*Speotyto cunicularia*

Threatening posture by burrowing owl on its nest. Both burrowing owls take turns at sitting on the eggs during a month long incubation period. The nesting chamber is usually at the end of a 5 ft long tunnel.

LW Walker

453

Burrowing toad

This is a single species of Mexican toad, also known as the digger toad, in a family on its own due to its many peculiarities. It is at most 2½ in. long, its body shaped almost like a hen's egg, its head small and ending in a pointed pig-like snout. It is dark brown with a yellow or orange stripe down the back and yellow spots on the flanks. Its skin is smooth and very thin. The burrowing toad is restricted to parts of Mexico and Guatemala. Its local name is poche *or* po-chi.

A shovel on its foot

The burrowing toad spends the day in holes in the ground, which it digs in wooded areas. Its eyes have the vertical pupils typical of nocturnal foragers, and these can expand in a dim light. It has no external signs of an ear, which is seen in most frogs and toads. When alarmed it blows itself up and starts moving backwards, using the hind feet in a digging action. This can best be appreciated when a burrowing toad is held in the hand. The horny shovel on the hind foot comes into play, to secure a hold. The shovel is at the base of the inner toe, which also has an enlarged tip used in digging.

Its voice has been described as guttural and more like the hoarse cry of a bird.

Catches termites with its tongue

Most toads and frogs have their tongue rooted at the front of the mouth and this shoots out to capture insects and must then be curled right back into the mouth each time. Another of the burrowing toad's peculiarities is that its tongue is more like our own, being rooted at the back. This is probably related to its feeding almost exclusively on termites, but the exact way it is used is not known.

Life history

The male usually calls on land, but breeding takes place in water, after heavy rains. At first the eggs are in a mass but after a while they separate and each floats on its own at the surface. The tadpoles have several long barbels or 'whiskers' around the mouth and they lack the lips found in other tadpoles. They are filter-feeders, their food being small algae and diatoms. The larval life is spent wholly in water and when 1 in. or more long the tadpole changes into the tailless toad.

How to fool a snake

Toads react more strongly to danger signals than frogs do, possibly because, not being leapers, they are more vulnerable and need added protection from enemies. One reaction is to inflate the lungs more than usual, so increasing the volume of the body by as much as 50%. Snakes, their chief enemies, know fairly accurately when an

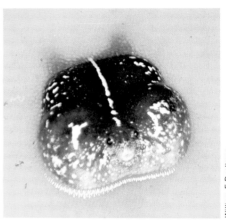

△ *When alarmed the burrowing toad blows itself up. It is an instinctive reaction to the presence of enemies.*

◁ *It is found in wooded areas of Mexico and Guatemala and feeds almost exclusively on termites. Breeding takes place in water after heavy rains.*

object is more than they can swallow, but how far the inflated body of the toad deceives them has never been tested.

Unless the snake is only small, the swelling of the toad will make little difference to the outcome if attacked by a constricting or a poisonous snake.

The defence mechanism of the toad of inflating itself against enemies is instinctive. This is seen by the following experiment. Any long cylindrical object, such as a length of thin rubber tubing or even a grass stalk, moved across its field of vision, will cause it to blow itself up once again, but not so strongly the second time. The third time it is less strong still, and in a short while no reaction is produced.

There is nothing clever about this defence mechanism. A toad has been seen to blow itself up when confronted by a bunch of wriggling worms and then, as the worms disentangle themselves and start to crawl away, the toad returns to normal and eats the worms one by one.

William E Duellman

class	**Amphibia**
order	**Salientia**
family	**Rhinophrynidae**
genus & species	***Rhinophrynus dorsalis***

Burying beetles

There are seven species of beetles in Britain known as burying, or sexton, beetles. The largest of these, about 1 in. long, is appropriately black all over. The others are black with orange bands. They are seldom seen except by those who turn over the decomposing corpse of a small bird or mouse lying on the ground.

Digging a mortuary chamber

Burying beetles pick up the odour of rotting flesh and home on it. They are strong on the wing and fly about by night, often being attracted to lights. They feed on dead animals. If the carcase is too large for burial the beetles will feed on it and depart, but if it is small enough, such as a small songbird, a mouse or a mole, they will set to work to bury it. Usually two, a male and a female, work together, and drive away any others flying to the carcase.

The beetles burrow under the carcase. They scrape earth away with the first pair of legs and throw it out to the sides with the two other pairs of legs. They do this in such a way that the carcase, in sinking into the ground, becomes folded on itself. As digging proceeds, earth thrown out by the beetles fills the space above. Eventually, at a depth of up to 8 in., a mortuary chamber slightly larger than the carcase has been excavated. Then the beetles strip the carcase of its fur or feathers using their jaws and mould and knead it into a ball. At this stage the female drives the male away.

A meal follows the dig

Once the male has left, the female returns to the ball of carrion, climbs on top of it and chews a hole in it from which to feed. It is her first meal since digging began.

In addition to feeding on putrefying flesh, burying beetles devour blowfly maggots. They will take these from a fly-blown carcase, carrying the maggots a short way away before eating them.

Feeding from mother's jaws

From the mortuary chamber the female beetle drives a long tunnel into the earth and lays her eggs at intervals in its wall. The eggs hatch in five days and as each larva emerges it makes its way to the mortuary chamber either along the tunnel or by burrowing to it through the earth. In the chamber, the larvae make their way to the female and put their jaws in the pit she has eaten in the carrion. They do not eat it, however, but wait for the female to come to them, when they raise their heads and take liquid from her jaws. She gives each in turn a drop of the brown liquid, the larvae struggling and competing with each other to reach it. This goes on for the first six hours of larval life, after which the larvae can feed themselves. They are fed again by the mother for a short while after the first two moults.

The larva of the burying beetle is unusual in that it changes its form at each of the three moults which precede the pupal stage. To pupate, each larva bores through the earth to about a foot away from the mortuary chamber.

About 1 in. long, the burying beetle feeds on dead animals usually bigger than itself. If the carcase is small enough the beetle buries it, usually with the help of a male, and then uses its powerful jaws to strip the carcase of its fur and mould and knead it into a ball.

Jane Burton, Photo Res.

Jane Burton. Photo Res.

Intelligent beetles

Some insects at times behave in ways that seem to us intelligent. Nevertheless, such is the low order of their brain (the two cerebral ganglia—nervous junctions in the head) and the rest of the nervous system that entomologists are unwilling to concede that they could be capable of intelligent acts. So we beg the question by saying they have 'plastic' behaviour. That is, while the things they do are almost entirely the result of what is usually called instinct, they can depart from these rigid lines of behaviour as and when circumstances demand.

Burying beetles show something of this plastic behaviour in dealing with the carcases they bury. When digging they may come across roots, which they bite through. If the carcase becomes entangled in grass, so failing to fall into the hole, the beetles will cut through the grass. This clearly indicates a recognition of a problem and a searching around for the means of solving it.

When experimentally someone has tied the carcase with string, to prevent it falling into the hole, the beetles have bitten through it. Even wire will not defeat them. The beetles try to sever it with their jaws and, failing, they sever the fastened limb.

Few entomologists would agree that beetles could perform actions requiring intelligence. Here, however, a shrew had a leg firmly tied with string so it could not be buried by a burying beetle. The beetle cut through the string so the shrew fell into the hole dug for it.

phylum	**Arthropoda**
class	**Insecta**
order	**Coleoptera**
family	**Silphidae**
genera	***Necrophorus,*** *others*

Bushbaby

Senegal bushbaby. It rests during the day, and feeds at night, catching insects or taking seeds and fruit or even birds' eggs. It is very agile, and can jump well over 10 ft while moving from tree to tree.

There are five species of bushbaby, or galago, all from Africa south of the Sahara. The most widespread and well-known is the Moholi, or Senegal galago, also known as the night-ape. The others are the dwarf, or Demidoff's galago, of tropical Africa, up to 13 in. long including an 8-in. tail, and the great galago, from East and South Africa, also known as the thick-tailed or large grey bushbaby, 2½ ft long, of which half is tail.

The last two are the rare Allen's galago of central West Africa and the needle-clawed galago, also of West Africa.

The bushbaby or Moholi galago— Pookie to South Africans—is 16 in. long including its long tail, which is bushy except at the base. It has a round head, short muzzle and large eyes. The ears, also, are large and flesh-coloured and can be folded at will. Its hind legs are long, the front legs shorter and its fur ranges

from yellowish-grey to brown. There is a varying amount of white on the muzzle and throat. The ends of the fingers and toes are flattened with pads of thick skin on the underside that give a grip on a smooth surface, and they have flattened nails.

Bushbabies belong to the suborder Prosimii, which includes the lemurs, so, although related to monkeys and apes, they are more primitive in character.

457

Prowling by night

Bushbabies live in groups, in dry scrub or bush. They rest together by day in dense foliage, in hollow trees, in a fork, or in an old bird's nest. At night, when they come out to feed, they move about singly or in pairs, their extreme activity and agility contrasting with their lethargic movements if disturbed by day. A bushbaby will take long leaps from branch to branch, with great agility and balance, covering as much as 15 ft in a leap. A standing jump upwards from the ground of 7 ft 4¾ in. has been recorded. On a level surface it may run on its hindlegs only. Bushbabies use their hands to pick up food or objects to examine them. They catch insects with their hands.

As in large primates, there is a good deal of grooming each other's fur and licking. Individuals greet each other with rasping notes. Aggression is shown by rising on the hindlegs and baring the teeth. Territory is marked by wetting feet and hands with urine, and similar use is said to be made of wet pawmarks, to mark a trail by which the individual finds its way back after a

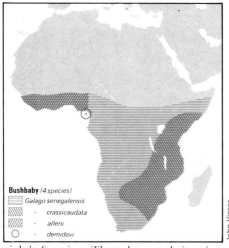

Bushbaby *(4 species)*
Galago senegalensis
    - *crassicaudata*
    - *alleni*
    - *demidovi*

night's foraging. They also use their voice to establish and advertise a territory, with high and low notes.

The characteristic sound of a bushbaby, the one responsible for its name, is a cry like that of a human baby. But one analysis of their sounds gives cackles and clicks, to draw attention to themselves, grunts and squeaks when apprehensive, sneezes and woofs when exploring, moans for distress, and shrieks when alarmed.

Mixed diet for all

Mainly insects, especially locusts, are eaten, but they will also take flowers, pollen, honey, seeds and fruits as well as birds' eggs, even unfledged nestlings.

Two breeding periods a year

There are two breeding periods in the year with 2 babies, rarely 1 or 3, in each, born April to November after a gestation of about 4 months. From the time it is born the mother carries her baby, by the nape, in her mouth. The baby can walk on all fours from the time it is born, can stand on its hindlegs at 24 hours and takes short leaps within a week. It begins taking solid food within 2 to 3 weeks, and is fully weaned at 7 to 10 weeks. The life-span is up to 10 years.

Pollination by mammals

The usual pollinators of flowers are insects, but there are instances of large animals that perform this task. The baobab, an African tree, with large white pendulous flowers 5 in. across, is visited by the straw-coloured fruit bat. Its flowers open after sunset to display many anthers which contain the male pollen grains, fertilising parts of a flower. The bats feed on the flowers with their faces buried among the anthers, and so they carry pollen from one flower to another, thus bringing about the fertilisation of another flower.

In East Africa, in 1964, MJ Coe and FM Isaac found that a group of bushbabies, known as the thick-tailed galagos, visited the baobabs on eight consecutive nights. They fed on the newly-opened flowers, moving from one to another, burying their faces in them. When the flowers fell the next day each showed signs of having been

licked and chewed and the small fleshy sepals almost completely eaten. In the light of a torch on subsequent nights the zoologists could see a pale ring around each bushbaby's face where the pollen dusted the fur. Although the animals were feeding on the flowers they were eating only the outer parts. The pistils remain undamaged.

class	**Mammalia**
order	**Primates**
family	**Lorisidae**
genus & species	***Galago alleni*** *Allen's bushbaby* **G. crassicaudatus** *thick-tailed bushbaby* **G. demidovi** *Demidoff's bushbaby* **G. senegalensis** *Senegal bushbaby* **Euoticus elegantulus** *needle-clawed galago*

▽ *Young bushbaby clinging to a branch waiting mother's return so it can ride on her back.*

▽▽ *Mother carrying her baby, holding it by the flank. The baby will take solid food at 1 month.*

Bushbuck

The bushbuck is the smallest antelope in the genus Tragelaphus *to which the nyala, kudu and situtunga also belong. It stands 28–30 in. high at the shoulder and weighs 100–170 lb. The colour of the back and flanks ranges from a light tawny in females to a dark brown in males. The males are usually darker underneath. There is a considerable amount of white on the body, including patches on the throat, two spots on the cheeks below the eyes and traces of white around lips and chin. White stripes run down the insides of the legs, and on the body there is a variety of spots and stripes running both down and along. The pattern of the spots and stripes varies greatly between the 20 or more subspecies.*

The males are distinctly larger than the females and have a bushy mane along the length of the back, which can be erected in fear or alarm, and a pair of sharp horns that may reach 22 in. Very occasionally females will bear horns. The spiral horns twist in rather more than one complete turn and have keels on both front and back. The old males often develop patches of hairless skin around the neck that make them look as if they have been wearing collars. These marks are made by the tips of the horns when they are thrown back as the bushbuck goes through thick undergrowth.

Solitary except in rut

Unlike most antelopes bushbuck lead solitary lives except during the rut and breeding season when buck and does or doe and calf will be seen together. They are not seen often as they tend to come out at dusk, although they enjoy sunbathing in the early morning. They have very sensitive hearing and eyesight, and in areas where they are often disturbed skilful stalking is needed to observe them. They are very adept at wending their way through dense undergrowth, and make use of low tunnels through the jungle undergrowth.

Bushbuck can make considerable leaps and will take to the water when pursued.

The bushbuck ranges across Africa from the shores of the Red Sea in Somalia and Ethiopia westward across the southern borders of the Sahara desert to Senegal, and south to the Cape Province of South Africa. Their home is forest and bush and they are absent only from open plains, deserts and ground more than 10 000 ft above sea-level. They are never too far from water to be able to drink once a day.

Browsing herbivores

Bushbuck are mainly browsers, feeding on leaves, the tips of twigs and such wild fruits as acacia pods and wild olives. They will occasionally graze—that is, feed on grass.

Breeding the year round

Calves are born all the year round, after a gestation of about 8 months, but most are born mid-October to mid-November.

△ *Young bushbuck ram,* Tragelaphus scriptus, *photographed on the banks of the Sabie River, Kruger National Park, South Africa.*

▽ *Young bushbuck calf in the undergrowth, well camouflaged by its colouring. Calves are born after a gestation of 8 months.*

Arthur Markowitz

Jane Burton, Photo Res.

△ *The male bushbuck, distinctly larger than the female, has a bushy mane along the length of the back.*
◁ *Bushbuck live in forest and bush of Africa feeding on leaves, the tips of twigs and wild fruits.*
▽ *Although calves are born all the year round most are born between mid-October and mid-November.*

AJ Sutcliffe

Phillippa Scott

Okapia

Tough in defence

Bushbuck bark, rather like a dog, when threatened or alarmed. Their main enemies are leopards and wild dogs. Lions are not a serious menace because they hunt in open country. Crocodiles have also been recorded as killing bushbuck, not only dragging them under as they come down to drink, but going on land to catch them as they feed. The predators do not find bushbuck an easy kill, for they are very stalwart in defence and have been known to kill both leopards and wild dogs, usually impaling them on their horns.

Pugnacious bushbuck

Although they are considerably smaller than their relatives in the genus *Tragelaphus*, bushbuck have established for themselves a reputation for being dangerous, especially when wounded. Their ability to move about rapidly through undergrowth gives them the edge over a hunter who has to force his way through the vegetation. It quite often happens that a hunter stalking a bushbuck through a thicket suddenly finds the tables turned and that he is the subject of an ambush.

Dogs are often used to flush the bushbuck but they are forced from cover only reluctantly. The males, especially, avoid coming out and will rather turn at bay, while the females and calves retreat to safety. Women and children first is often the order of the day in the family Bovidae, where the males deliberately place themselves between females and young and the enemy. With their sharp horns and hooves they have often been known to kill dogs and will even chase, and have been known to kill, men, especially when wounded.

It is not only the horned males that are to be feared. Theodore Roosevelt, the American traveller and hunter, recorded that one of his beaters was knocked flat by a charging bushbuck doe.

class	**Mammalia**
order	**Artiodactyla**
family	**Bovidae**
genus & species	***Tragelaphus scriptus***

▷ *Bushbuck caught by the photographer's flash.*

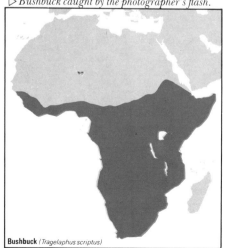

Bushbuck *(Tragelaphus scriptus)*

Peter Ward

This South American stockily built dog apparently spends the day in deserted armadillo burrows, coming out at night to hunt for food.

Bushdog

This is a South American member of the dog family, only distantly related to the domestic dog but behaving very like it when tamed. The bushdog is up to 15 in. at the shoulder. Its fur is brown, with the head, neck and forequarters orange, tawny or white, the belly, hindquarters and tail dark brown, almost black. There are sometimes lighter patches on various parts of the body. Stocky in build, with very short legs, it has a longish coat and an almost brush-like tail. The species was first described from sub-fossil bones found in Brazilian caves.

Wide-ranging but elusive

The bushdog is seldom seen, although it ranges from Panama to the northern half of South America, from eastern Peru to the Guianas and south to Paraguay. It lives in woodlands and grassy plains where the soil is sandy, but, being nocturnal, usually eludes even those who seek it. It is said to spend the day in deserted armadillo burrows. Descriptions of the calls of the bushdog suggest that its vocabulary is similar to that of the red fox. The cry is said to

include whines, squeals, dog-like barks and almost bird-like noises.

The outstanding feature of the bushdog is its fondness for water. It is a skilful swimmer and diver, able to swim under water, and a tame one not only retrieved sticks thrown into water but would dive to the bottom and bring up stones thrown in for it to retrieve.

Hunts in gangs

The bushdog, like other members of the Canidae, probably eats any flesh, dead or alive, and a proportion of plant matter, including soft fruits. All we know about its diet is the repeated report that it hunts the paca, a heavily-built, 2-ft long rodent of tropical America. A pack of bushdogs will pursue the paca into water. While some bushdogs chase it through the water, others line the bank to effect a kill should the paca escape its swimming pursuers. In the London Zoo, one bushdog is fed 1 lb. of meat on the bone a day.

Bred in zoos

Virtually nothing is known about the breeding of bushdogs. Litters of four and five have been recorded in the San Diego Zoo. In the wild, a pregnant female was seen swimming across the Rio Negro with two youngsters accompanying her.

Not all dogs swim

Although we divide animals into terrestrial and aquatic species, there are few land animals that fail to swim if pressed to do so, and among typical terrestrial animals there are usually some individuals that will do so for the fun of it. Domestic dogs show a fondness for water, so it should not be surprising to find the bushdog, too, likes water. There is one breed of domestic dog, the Portuguese water dog, which not only swims and dives well but can be trained to retrieve fishing gear lost on the bed of the sea. At the other end of the scale there are sometimes individual dogs that not only fail to swim but cannot be taught to do so. One boxer dog, some years ago, would enter water but refused to swim; even the patient efforts of a skilled trainer produced no result in this direction.

class	**Mammalia**
order	**Carnivora**
family	**Canidae**
genus & species	***Speothos venaticus***

463

The bushpig digs with its snout for roots, causing much damage to cultivated crops in Africa.

Zool. Soc. Lond.

Bushpig

The bushpig, known in West Africa as red river hog and in South Africa as bosvark, ranges over Africa south of the Sahara and is found in Madagascar. It is stout-bodied, with a coat of short bristles and with longer, wiry bristles along the mid line of the back and neck, on the sides of the face and the lower flanks. The head is disproportionately large, the muzzle is narrow, the ears run to a point and are tufted. There is a pair of warts on the face below the eyes, larger in old individuals but in most of them inconspicuous because of the long hairs on the face. The bushpig's colour varies. Young adults are rufous red and this changes with increased age to reddish-brown or black, especially on the shoulders and legs. The long bristles of the face and the crest of the back are a mixed white and black, the white predominating in some, the black in others. There is often much white on the face.

The head and body measure up to 4 ft; the slender tail, with its double tuft of bristles at the tip, measuring 1 ft. The height at the shoulder averages 2½ ft. The weight is up to 300 lb. The tusks are not obvious while the mouth is shut. The upper tusk is 3 in. long, the lower tusk is 7½ in. long. The upper tusk rubs on the lower, keeping both sharp through a kind of honing action.

Boss boar and page

The typical habitat is broken country with patches of forest or thicket, reed beds or well-wooded rocky ravines, always where water is readily available for drinking and there is mud for wallowing. Bushpigs roll a good deal, in mud or in grass, and they rub their flanks against chosen trees and gash the bark of these with their tusks. It has been suggested that this may serve as a territorial marker.

Bushpigs are highly secretive and rarely show themselves. Mainly nocturnal, they come out by day only when they are completely undisturbed. Even then, they rapidly make for cover at the first alarm.

Bushpigs live in 'sounders' made up of an old boar, two or more sows and young of varying ages. One of the younger adult boars exercises control when the boss boar is away. European wild boars similarly have a dominant boar with a 'page'. A sounder may number as few as four or as many as twenty.

Bushpigs run fast, swim well and show a spirited defence against intruders, both of their own and other species, the first signs of aggression being the raising of the bristles on the back. They are said to be very shy of traps.

Topples trees for food

Their main food is roots and wild fruits, but like the domestic pig they will readily eat flesh, including eggs and young birds. To obtain the fruits from small trees, bushpigs will lean heavily against the trunks to topple the trees.

Leopards the main enemy

Because of the pig's strength, sharp tusks and belligerent disposition, enemies are few, probably restricted to lions and leopards, which may kill the young. Leopards are probably the main enemy, but there are records of leopards treed by the hostile actions of several adult bushpigs.

Litter in a bower

The gestation period is unknown. Farrowing occurs from the end of September to the end of March, with a peak in December and January, usually in periods of rains. The sow makes a 'bower' in long grass for her litter. The young, when first born, are brown with yellowish longitudinal stripes, later turning rufous brown. A litter includes 2–6 young, occasionally 8, and as many as 10 has been recorded, although the sow has only three pairs of teats. A bushpig has lived 14 years 8 months in captivity, but they may live as much as 20 years.

Destructive cultivator

Bushpigs are a menace to cultivated crops, especially since their enemies the leopards have become scarce through being hunted. It is not only the amount they eat and trample underfoot, but the damage they do by rooting with the snout–the bushpig's characteristic way of searching for food–and ploughing through the crops. The situation is not helped by the animal's secret habits and elusiveness and by the ineffectiveness of dogs as guardians. A bushpig is robust, heavy and full of fighting spirit, and these qualities combined with the slashing use of the razor-sharp teeth are enough to send any dog packing.

C Astley Maberly has suggested that it is just those features of the bushpig's behaviour which infuriate farmers that make it a valuable cultivator in wild country. It ploughs the land especially during the rainy season, loosening and aerating the soil, speeding up the decomposition of dead branches and twigs by cutting them up with its hoofs and trampling them into the churned-up soil, and fertilizing the ground and dispersing seeds with its droppings. The wild fig is completely dependent on the bushpig's cultivations as it bears its fruits underground. The bushpig digs out the fruit with its snout, eats and scatters the undigested seeds over the land.

class	**Mammalia**
order	**Artiodactyla**
family	**Suidae**
genus & species	***Potamochoerus porcus***

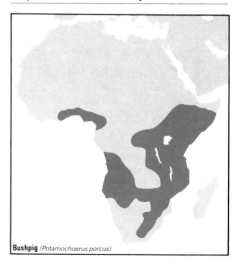

Bushpig *(Potamochoerus porcus)*

Bustard

Bustards are large-bodied birds, 14 – 52 in. long, with stout legs and blunt, strong toes suited for swift running. The great bustard is as large as a turkey, weighing up to 32 lb with an 8-ft wingspan. The head and bill are flattened and there are often ornamental plumes on head and neck. Males are frequently larger than females and differ in plumage, which is generally grey or brown with black and white markings. There are 22 species of bustard.

Shy birds

Bustards live in open country such as plains, downs and deserts, where their mottled plumage camouflages them and they can run freely on their powerful legs.

Some species form small parties outside the breeding season, others are solitary. They are very shy birds. Gilbert White records that great bustards took flight when he was about ½ mile away. Later writers give the shorter distance of 500 yds. In view of this extreme timorousness it is not surprising that great bustards no longer breed on the downlands of southern England or the brecks of East Anglia.

They are found in many parts of the Old World from the Canaries to Australia, with most species living in Africa. Many of them now have a reduced range because of over-hunting. The great bustard used to live in Britain but ceased to breed there about 1830. It is still found in other parts of Europe as well as in Asia. The little bustard is still found in southwestern Europe. The great Indian bustard of northwest India is now very rare and the Australian bustard is also in a perilous state.

Australian bustard kills snakes

Animal and plant material, including crops such as cereals, cabbages and peas, are taken. The young birds feed mainly on insects. Adults will swallow field-voles, frogs, lizards and nestling skylarks.

The Australian bustard, or plain turkey, often kills and eats small snakes. The snakes are caught in the bill and banged against the hard, horny toes until immobile, then swallowed. Sometimes the snakes are regurgitated and given a further thrashing before being re-swallowed.

Courtship transformation

Many of the bustards have striking courtship displays, involving the plumes, inflatable air sacs and ruffling of the plumage. The male Australian bustard fluffs out the feathers on its throat and back and inflates from its throat a great fold of feather-covered skin which hangs down to the ground. At the same time it utters a booming note that sounds from a distance like a roaring lion.

The male of the great bustard undergoes a remarkable transformation when it displays. From being a rather dull grey and brown bird it suddenly becomes a billowing mass of white feathers. The feathers on the back are turned over, and the tail is turned up and over the back, to display their white undersides. At the same time, the head sinks onto the shoulders, the moustache-like bristly, white feathers on the cheeks stand upright and the air sac under the throat is inflated. As the legs are bent and the wings fluffed out, it looks like an untidy ball of feathers.

Bustards make very little in the way of a nest, merely trampling a patch in the grass or scraping a depression in the ground. The female incubates the eggs. Sometimes the male will stand nearby, but some species are promiscuous, the male and female going their separate ways after mating. The eggs, from 1 – 5 in number, according to the species, hatch in about 1 month and the chicks can leave the nest and run about as soon as they are dry. The female looks after them for another month or more, at first

The great bustard performs a strange courtship dance. From being a sombre grey and brown bird it suddenly becomes a billowing mass as the feathers of the back are turned over.

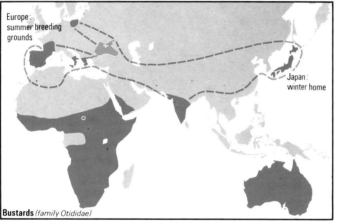

△ *Little bustard,* Otis tetrax, *of northern Africa and Eurasia nests in south-western Europe. The colour of the bird blends with the surroundings as it nests on the ground.*

▽ *Great bustard,* O. tarda, *is one of the largest flying birds in the world. It can reach a weight of about 30 lb and a length of 52 in.*

Europe: summer breeding grounds

Japan: winter home

Bustards *(family Otididae)*

catching insects to give them in her bill. Later the chicks can catch their own insects, but they stay with their mother until they have learnt to fly.

Before they can fly, it appears that the mother bustard can carry the chicks to safety on her back. At least, it is recorded that the Australian bustard will do so. On one occasion two men tried to catch a young bustard but its mother crouched down, spread her tail like a fan so that the chick could run onto her back and then flew off with it. This sounds incredible but there are records of other species of birds carrying their young pick-a-back.

The human menace

Despite their wariness and their ability to carry their young to safety, bustards fall prey to many enemies, as do the majority of ground-nesting birds. Foxes will kill both adults and young, and crows take eggs. As so often happens, however, man is their worst enemy. A bustard the size of a chicken or turkey makes a good meal, so they are regularly hunted for the pot. This has led to their elimination from many parts of their former ranges. One trick used to overcome their shyness was to fix up several shotguns with strings running from their triggers. The hunter could then retire to a discreet distance and wait for the bustards to gather around the bait put in front of the guns.

Shot out of existence

At one time bustards were thought to have been brought to the British Isles by the Romans. This opinion was based on the absence of any fossil remains in these islands, but the Roman invaders have been erroneously credited with introducing so many things that we can probably dismiss it. Whatever the origin of the British bustards, it is certain they no longer exist. The last record of their breeding here was in Suffolk in 1832, while a few individuals held on until 1838 but without breeding. The bustard was too great an attraction to a man with a gun to be able to survive for long, especially in the face of the spread of agriculture.

Some attempt was made to preserve the bustards, but as game birds to be shot only by the wealthy, and it was only the Protection of Birds Act 1956 that removed the bustard from the list of British birds for which a game licence was needed.

Rigged up shotguns have been recorded as killing seven bustards in one blast, but the fortunes of battle sometimes went the other way. In 1751 the Rev W Chaffin, out shooting dotterel, disturbed a group of bustards. The reverend gentleman followed them on horseback and came almost within shot of them. When they flew up again, the noise of their wings startled the horse which reared up and galloped away, leaving the luckless clergyman on the ground.

class	**Aves**
order	**Gruiformes**
family	**Otididae**
genera & species	***Ardeotis australis*** *Australian bustard* ***Otis tarda*** *great bustard, others*

Butcherbird

The name butcherbird, which is also used for the shrikes, refers to the rather bloodthirsty habit of both birds of impaling their prey on thorns. The six butcherbirds of Australia and New Guinea, together with the currawongs and bell-magpies, also of Australia, make up a family that bears some resemblance to the crows and the shrikes.

They are stocky birds, about 10—23 in. long, with large heads and hooked, shrike-like bills. Like the rest of the family, the butcherbirds' plumage is mainly black and white. The grey butcherbird, or 'Whistling Jack', has a black face, neck and nape, grey back, rump and undersides, with blackish-brown and white wings and tail. The female is generally more brown on the upper parts. The black-throated or pied butcherbird, sometimes known as the 'Break o' Day Boy', is magpie-like with a glossy black head and neck, black back and black and white wings and tail. The female is brown on the back.

The shrikes belong to the family Laniidae. This mainly Old World family is made up of true shrikes, bush shrikes, helmet shrikes and bristleheads. The ordinary cry of the shrike is apt to be harsh and discordant— hence the name—but on the whole they are good or moderate songsters. Shrikes are characterised by a strong hooked bill. They are bold and aggressive birds, essentially carnivorous. Some species catch only insects, others add small amphibians, reptiles, birds and mammals.

Range

The black-headed and white-rumped butcherbirds are restricted to New Guinea; two others, the black and the black-backed, are found both in New Guinea and Northern Australia. The grey butcherbird ranges over most of Australia and Tasmania. It prefers the open forests around the coasts or the thickly-timbered mountain ranges, but is also found inland, in the woods that are scattered over the plains. The pied butcherbird is also widespread but lives more inland and is nowhere common. It is usually seen in twos, for butcherbirds stay paired all the year round, in open forest, pine scrub and the timber clumps on the plains.

Beautiful songster

Butcherbirds are shy creatures but become tame near human dwellings. Here they are welcomed for their lilting cheerful song, composed of long phrases repeated in different orders. The song bears no relation to the song of any European bird, except perhaps to the liquid phrases of a blackbird. The pied butcherbird was once described as chanting, slowly and richly, 'This is the tree', but this does not convey the beauty of the song. Male and female sing equally well and often perform duets. The song can be heard all the year round, and is often heard on moonlit nights. In the autumn and

Graham Pizzey NHPA

△ Australian grey butcherbird, Cracticus torquatus, about to feed a wasp to its fledgling.   ▽ Both Australian butcherbirds and some shrikes will impale prey on thorns or barbed wire.

H Schünemann

H Schünemann

The great grey shrike, Lanius excubitor, *about to swoop down on prey it has detected on the ground. This species is found over much of Europe, Asia and North America. Most shrikes are bold and aggressive and essentially carnivorous, catching insects, small amphibians, reptiles, birds, and mammals.*

winter, the song changes and is less sustained.

An unusual piece of behaviour was once observed at a sheep station in New South Wales. Dead sheep were found with all their exposed wool plucked out and rolled into pellets that lay scattered about. The pellets were the size of a pea and nearly as hard. Eventually this unusual happening was explained. A grey butcherbird was seen pulling at the wool, and as a tuft came loose it fell over backwards and lay on its back bundling the wool with its bill and feet. However, no explanation could be given as to why the butcherbird should do this. There seems to be no reason for it and it cannot be related to any normal behaviour, so the observation must join the many other pieces of animal behaviour that are seen only rarely and for which there is no explanation.

The butcherbird's larder
Butcherbirds live on large insects such as beetles, crickets and grasshoppers, small lizards, snakes, fieldmice and a few small birds. They pounce on insects and birds while they are on the ground, rather than when they are flying. This is done from some favoured look-out post, such as a branch or telephone wire. Surplus food is stored by impaling it on thorns, or in some cases wedging corpses of lizards into a tree-crotch, between trunk and branch. A

butcherbird has also been seen to drag a fledgling honeyeater along the jagged end of a broken branch so that it lodged there and was held firm while the butcherbird ripped off the flesh.

Surprisingly, butcherbirds are a nuisance to bird fanciers. They will fly to a cage of canaries or some other bird, causing them to panic. As one lands on the wire netting beside the butcherbird, it is grabbed and dragged through the mesh. The best protection against this predation is a double layer of netting.

Promiscuous relatives
Both male and female butcherbirds guard their territory by singing and chasing intruders. The territory may be defended all the year round, but during the breeding season defence becomes vigorous, and the predators such as snakes and ravens are attacked, as are humans. The year-round pairing of the butcherbirds contrasts with the behaviour of their near relatives the bell-magpies in which clans of up to 20 birds defend a large communal territory. There is no pairing and mating is promiscuous.

The butcherbird's nest is an untidy structure of twigs, lined with fibrous roots or grasses. It is about 9 in. in diameter with a 2-in. deep cup, and is placed usually 9–20 ft up in a tree. Sometimes the nest is so thinly built that the eggs can be seen

through the bottom.

Eggs number 3 or 4, sometimes 5. In dry parts, the pied butcherbird lays only one egg. They are incubated for 23 days and the chicks fledge after 25 or 26 days.

What is a songbird?
Australian birds are not noted for their songs but the butcherbirds stand out, the pied butcherbird being considered one of the world's best singers. It may seem rather strange that a flesh-eating, magpie-like bird should be a songbird, as one tends to think of songbirds as the familiar insect- and seed-eating garden birds such as blackbirds, robins, finches and wrens, along with larks and buntings. So the question arises as to whether the generally-used term 'songbird' covers any bird with a song, or whether it defines a certain group of birds, or whether the two are the same.

First, what is a song? It can be limited to sounds uttered in a regular and rhythmic fashion, but, on the other hand, 'song' is a term used by ornithologists to describe calls that have a definite function, such as to advertise the presence of a bird in its territory and so deter other males and encourage females. The calls used by gulls have the same function but they are hardly musical, and one would not describe a gull as a songbird. So, although many different birds can be said to have a song,

468

Great grey shrike with its 'larder', which is presumably to enable it to dispatch prey more easily. It perhaps also creates a reserve store when much prey has been caught. This shrike and the lesser great shrike, L. minor, *hover in a similar manner to some birds-of-prey such as the falcon.*

the term 'songbird' is usually limited to the sub-order Oscines of the order Passeriformes. This includes the familiar songbirds as well as bulbuls, mockingbirds and babblers. It also includes such less likely candidates as crows, shrikes and nuthatches. The basis for this distinction lies in the anatomy of the syrinx. This is the 'voicebox', having the same function as the larynx of animals. It lies in the windpipe and has a resonating chamber and vocal chords, whose tension is altered by special muscles to form different noises. The sub-order Oscines differs from other birds in having a more complex system of control, involving 5–9 pairs of muscles, thus allowing a wide variation in the sounds that can be produced.

class	**Aves**
order	**Passeriformes**
family	**Cracticidae**
genus & species	***Cracticus torquatus*** *grey butcherbird* **C. nigrogularis** *pied butcherbird* **C. cassicus** *black-headed butcherbird* **C. louisiadensis** *white-rumped butcherbird* **C. mentalis** *black-backed butcherbird* **C. quoyi** *black butcherbird*

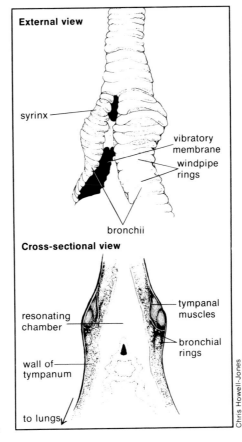

External view

syrinx

vibratory membrane

windpipe rings

bronchii

Cross-sectional view

resonating chamber

tympanal muscles

bronchial rings

wall of tympanum

to lungs

△ *Fiscal shrike,* L. collaris, *feeding its young in the nest built in a bunch of bananas.*
◁ *Butcherbird syrinx or 'voice box'. This typical syrinx resembles a set of bagpipes with the pipes cut off short. The lower rings of the windpipe form the resonating chamber (comparable with the bag of the bagpipes), at the fork of the two bronchii which convey air to the lungs (the pipes). When wind is expelled from the lungs it passes over the stretched membranes causing them to vibrate and thus produce various sounds. The membranes are controlled by muscles which can alter their tension and also move the windpipe.*

469

Butterfish

The butterfish is an eel-like blenny living between tide-marks on the North Atlantic coasts, as far south as the English Channel in the east and Wood's Hole, USA, in the west. Alternative names for it are gunnel and nine-eyes, from the row of dark spots along the back. The butterfish, up to 6 in. long, is ribbon-shaped, with a low dorsal fin running the length of the back, a long low anal fin, a small tail and very small paired fins. The body, coloured yellowish-green with darker markings, is covered with very small scales. The snout is short, and the teeth are very small.

'Butterfish' refers to the slippery nature of the fish and the difficulty one has in holding it between the fingers. Another name is butter-eel. Since this is a characteristic of many fishes it is not surprising to find a New Zealand wrasse also called a butterfish, as well as two other unrelated species in coastal waters of the United States, all of which have slimy bodies.

Meat eaters

Little is known of feeding in the natural state but butterfish kept in aquaria take shreds of meat and small invertebrates of various kinds, suggesting a wide diet, mainly carnivorous.

Eggs rolled into a ball

Spawning is from December to March. The female lays her eggs in a mass, usually in a cavity in a rock or in an empty bivalve shell. The egg-mass's diameter is a little over 1 in. The female curves her body into a loop while laying, so rolling the egg-mass into a ball. Once the mass is laid the male coils himself round it and continues to protect the eggs in this way until they hatch. The usual explanation for this is that the eggs are sticky only when first laid, and the parent's action in rolling the body round the mass is to prevent them from becoming scattered. It is unusual for marine fishes to show this amount of parental care. It is even more rare for the female to take turns with the male, as the butterfish is reputed to do.

The eggs hatch more than a month after laying, the larvae being $\frac{2}{5}$ in. long. They drift out to sea and spend several months at depths of about 190 ft before returning to the shallow coastal waters.

Very united family

The protective membrane around each egg is so fragile that it is almost impossible to remove one from the mass without rupturing it. This is probably why such devotion is needed from the parents. If the eggs became separated, the chances of their surviving would be negligible. There may, nevertheless, be another need for their being kept together in a mass.

Experiments carried out on other species in which eggs are laid in masses suggest that each egg helps the development of the others. That is, they must keep together for the common good. In one experiment, some eggs from a mass were carefully separated one by one and put in separate aquaria. The remainder were left in an aquarium on their own, still tightly packed. All had similar water, air, and light. The separated eggs either failed to hatch or the larvae from them were deformed.

class	**Osteichthyes**
order	**Perciformes**
family	**Pholidae**
genus & species	*Pholis gunnellus*

Uncovered at low tide

The butterfish, like other blennies, is most commonly seen when the tide is out, sheltering under stones or seaweeds, or in rock crevices kept damp by overhanging seaweeds. When disturbed it darts rapidly through the water of a rock pool, or wriggles over the wet stones or seaweeds. It becomes more active when, at high tide, it is completely covered with water. Moreover, as with other blennies (see p. 373), butterfish living close inshore alternate active periods with resting periods, corresponding with the rise and fall of the tide.

△ *The butterfish is a 6 in. eel-like blenny.*

▽ *The name refers to its very slippery skin.*

470

The freshwater butterfly fish Pantodon buchholzi *found in the waters of western Africa is one of the strangest of the so-called flying fishes. It spends most of its time swimming just under the surface and is capable of leaping out of the water for a distance of 6 or more feet.*

Butterfly fish

It is virtually impossible to speak about butterfly fishes without confusion since the name is commonly used for different kinds of unrelated fishes. The same can be said of angelfishes. Attention has already been drawn to this on page 131, where some butterfly fishes have been described, together with their very close relatives, the marine angelfishes. Here we return to this subject to deal with a freshwater fish that has also been described as a butterfly fish. At the same time this gives us the opportunity to contrast and compare it with the marine fishes, inhabitants of coral reefs especially, which are also called butterfly fishes. For our description of the habits of marine butterfly fishes we must refer to page 131. But here on the next two pages we portray these fishes, belonging to the family Chaetodontidae, in a series of fascinating and beautiful photographs.

The one species of freshwater butterfly fish is sufficiently extraordinary to merit close attention on its own. Never more than 4 in. long, it lives in the rivers of tropical West Africa. Its head and body are boat-shaped, flattened above, bluntly rounded below. It is coloured grey-green to brownish-silver, marked with spots and streaks. The large mouth is directed upwards, and the nostrils are tubular. Another remarkable feature is its fins. The pectoral fins are large and wing-like. Each pelvic fin has four very long filamentous rays not connected to each other, and the unpaired fins are large, transparent and supported by long rays.

For a long time the relationships of this fish, first discovered in 1876, have been in doubt, but it is now placed in a family on its own near that of the large South American fish, the arapaima. It has no relationship with the marine butterfly fishes of the family Chaetodontidae.

A fish that flies

This remarkable fish is reckoned to fly over the water, flapping its wings like a bat or a bird. The freshwater butterfly fish spends most of its time just below the surface of still or stagnant waters in the Congo and Niger basins, in the weedy backwaters and standing pools. But it is most renowned for its ability to leap out of water for distances up to 6 ft, its large pectoral fins being used, as are those of the true flying fishes, in gliding flight. It has also been credited with flapping these fins in true powered flight, as in bats and birds. By 1960, however, it had been generally agreed that this was not so.

Then came a remarkable sequel. PH Greenwood and KS Thomson investigated the anatomy of this fish. They found it had a most unusual shoulder girdle, the arrangement of bones to which the pectoral fins are attached. In fact, these two authors described it as unique among fishes. The bones were so thin that they had to be very careful not to damage them while dissecting them out. The whole of the shoulder girdle is broad and flattened to give support to a highly developed system of muscles, comparable with the large pectoral muscles that work the wings of birds. The two scientists also found that the fins could not be folded against the body, as is usual in fishes, but could be moved up and down. In brief, they concluded that, while it was still unproven whether or not the butterfly fish could make a powered flight, its shoulder girdle and muscles were such that it ought to be able to fly. The best that can be said is that the fish has been seen to beat its fins up and down when held in the hand. It has, however, been suggested that this is only used to

Gene Wolfsheimer

△ *Vividly-striped marine butterfly fishes are deep-bodied and flattened from side to side.*

▽ *The freshwater butterfly fish is not related to marine butterfly fishes of the tropical seas.*

▽▽ *Four-eyed butterfly fish, so-called because of the false 'eye' markings at its tail end.*

AC Wheeler AFA

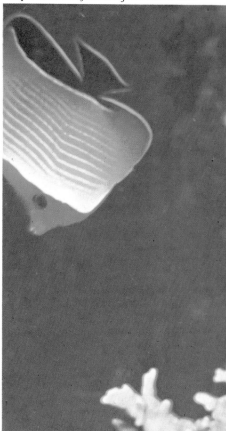

Douglas Faulkner

Douglas Faulkner

give the butterfly fish a push-off from the water to become airborne.

Insect feeder

The food consists almost entirely of the small insects, such as flies, that fall onto the surface of the water.

Life history

Relatively little is known about the breeding, and such details as we have are from the few butterfly fishes that have bred in captivity. Numerous false matings have been seen, with the male riding on the back of the female, sometimes for hours at a time, holding her firmly with the long rays of the pelvic fins. Mating finally is effected by the two twisting their bodies together to bring

▽ *Marine butterfly fishes* Chaetodon *live around coral reefs in shallow tropical seas.*

Similarly, it may be some years before we can be sure whether the West African butterfly fishes beat their wings or not. There is, however, one group of freshwater fishes that do beat their fins to achieve true flight through the air. These are the hatchet fishes of northern South America, found from the River Plate to Panama.

As so often happens, another confusion of names arises. We already have it over butterfly fishes, as we have seen. There are also two kinds of hatchet fishes. One kind is marine (see page 1174) and the other is freshwater. They both get their names from their shape, the body being flattened from side to side, so that it looks like the blade of a hatchet.

The freshwater hatchet fishes beat their pectoral fins rapidly when making a take-off run over the surface before becoming airborne, and they continue to beat their fins when airborne.

To make the confusion even more confounded, it may be mentioned that freshwater hatchet fishes do a butterfly-like dance during their courtship. Fortunately we can note the scientific names and there can be no doubt as to the animal referred to. Each animal has a binomial name of genus and species, rather like the surname and christian name used to identify humans.

class	**Osteichthyes**
order	**Osteoglossiformes**
family	**Pantodontidae**
genus & species	*Pantodon buchholzi* *freshwater butterfly fish*

▽ *The butterfly fish* Heniochus acuminatus *lives in the warm seas around the Philippine Islands. It has a very deep body, most of the depth being due to a highly arched back.*

the vents opposite each other. Fertilisation seems, therefore, to be internal. As soon as they are laid the eggs float to the surface, and in 3 days these hatch. The fry remain at the surface feeding on the tiniest of the insects, such as springtails and aphides, which fall on it.

To beat or not to beat

The ability to make either gliding or powered flights through the air is rare among fishes, although to be able to leap from the water is common enough. For years, scientists have argued among themselves whether or not the flying fishes of the oceans beat their wings when airborne. At present, evidence suggests that they do not.

Buttonquail

Buttonquails are small birds, 4 – 7 in. long, resembling true quails both in appearance and habits. They are thought to be related to sandgrouse and pigeons. They have only three toes on each foot, the hind toe being missing. The wings are rounded and the tail so short as to be almost invisible. Buttonquails are sometimes called hemipodes and these names are often used to refer to the single European species.

Freezing in the grass

Buttonquails are very secretive, hiding among the undergrowth in pairs or small

Norman Chaffer

parties. Their home is dry bush or open country, sometimes open woodland or marshy areas. Observation of their habits and attempts to find their nests are made difficult because they are hard to flush, and then fly only weakly for a short distance over the grass. Once flushed, they are difficult to locate and put up again, for when they have landed after a disturbance, the buttonquails freeze. Then, if the danger appears to have passed, they creep away slowly through the vegetation, walking on the tips of their toes.

Buttonquails are found in many parts of the Old World. The striped buttonquail or Andalusian hemipode ranges from Spain, where it is rare, across Asia to the Philippines and throughout most of Africa, except the Sahara Desert and the tropical forests of the Congo basin. Other buttonquails live in Madagascar and the Australasian regions, including New Guinea, Melanesia and Mindanao in the Philippines.

Feeding

Buttonquails live on grass seeds, young shoots and insects which they scratch from the ground or find among the undergrowth.

Reversal of roles

Except for mating and egg-laying, the roles of the sexes in courtship and rearing offspring have been reversed in the buttonquails. The female is often more brightly coloured, and during the breeding season she calls to attract the male. The call of the striped buttonquail is a booming, heard most frequently at dawn and dusk. In Spain the bird is known as the torillo, or little bull, because of the resemblance of the call to the distant lowing of cattle. Guy Mountfort, in *Portrait of a Wilderness*, quotes an old peasant as saying that the buttonquail 'blows itself up in a ball and calls like a bull, but it keeps its mouth shut and the sound comes out of its ears'. In fact she has a special organ to produce the booming, formed by the inflation of the throat and windpipe, that acts as a resonator.

Having attracted a male, the female then courts him. She struts round in a circle with tail raised and chest puffed out, at the same time booming, stamping and pecking at the ground. At the end of courtship the roles of the sexes revert to the more normal pattern for mating to take place.

Sometimes the female builds the nest, while at other times both sexes join in, bringing grass and dead leaves to the site and flicking them over their shoulders towards the growing pile of material. In some species, such as the black-breasted buttonquail of Australia, the nest is no more than a scantily-lined depression in the ground. Others form a roof over the nest by drawing stems of grass together to make a dome. Occasionally a porch is added.

After the eggs, usually 4 in number, have been laid, the female deserts the nest and leaves the male to incubate them. They hatch in 12 or 13 days, and almost immediately the young can follow their male parent about while he searches for food, which he presents to them in his bill. In 2 weeks the chicks can fly but they stay together as a family for another fortnight. It is very unusual for birds with such a short incubation

time to be so well-developed and active soon after birth. Chicks spending less than a fortnight in the egg are usually blind, naked and helpless at birth.

Buttonquails also mature early, being able to breed in their fourth or fifth month.

Avian amazons

The changed roles of the sexes is shown by their plumage. The male buttonquail generally has drab plumage; fitting for a bird that has to sit as inconspicuously as possible on the nest. The female is often larger and more brightly coloured. The female of the barred bustardquail even acquires a courtship plumage in the breeding season.

The females are also belligerent, fighting among themselves as do the males of other species. In India, the females of the bustard-

◁ *Male painted quail* Turnix varia *at nest. Unlike most birds, it is the female who does the courting, using a special call and dance. After laying her eggs she deserts the nest, leaving the male to do the incubating.*

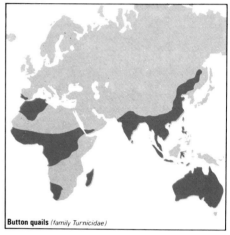

Button quails *(family Turnicidae)*

quail are trapped with decoys, models painted to look like female bustardquails. The females so caught are then set against each other as in cock-fighting.

As if to emphasise the relegation of the male to the female's traditional domestic role, the female buttonquail has several 'husbands'. Having provided one with a nest and eggs to look after she then departs to court another. For the male to mate with several females, each having her own nest and clutch, is not unusual among birds, but for a female to have several clutches is most surprising, because the difficulty of getting enough food to form the eggs usually limits the size of the clutch. It seems that the female buttonquails must have access to a very abundant food supply.

class	**Aves**
order	**Gruiformes**
family	**Turnicidae**
genus & species	***Turnix sylvatica*** *striped buttonquail* ***T. melanogaster*** *blackbreasted buttonquail* ***T. suscitator*** *barred bustardquail others*

Buzzard

This is a large hawk with soaring flight, distinguishable by its broad wings and rounded tail. Most of the many species of buzzards are found in open country in the tropics. All are large, with wing-spans of 3 – 5 ft. The female is larger than the male.

The common buzzard of Europe, averaging just under 2 ft long, also ranges across northern Asia to Japan, occupying a wide variety of habitats, from farmland to mountains and rocky coasts.

Other buzzards include the rough-legged buzzard of Scandinavia and Russia which regularly appears along the eastern coast of Britain during the winter, and the augur or jackal buzzard of Africa which occurs up to 17 000 ft. In America, members of the genus Buteo are named 'hawks', while 'buzzard' is popularly used to describe vultures. The honey-buzzards belong to the genus Pernis.

Effortless flight

Buzzards are well-known for their soaring flight, in which they circle around in great spirals, with wings outstretched and the primary wing feathers separated like fingers. British buzzards do not migrate but young buzzards sometimes travel across the country after leaving their parents. In Scandinavia buzzards migrate across the Baltic for the winter. The buzzards circle in rising air currents or thermals up to several hundred feet until they are mere

Common European buzzard bringing a rabbit to its waiting brood. The prey is caught and killed with the long, curved and sharp claws or talons on each of the four toes.

specks in the sky. Then they glide away across the country until they find another thermal to soar in. In this way buzzards can travel many miles without expending energy on flapping flight. It is common for birds of prey on migration to use this form of travel, especially when crossing a narrow strip of water such as the Straits of Dover or Gibraltar. They climb as high as possible over the coast, then glide across the water where there are few, if any, thermals.

The common buzzard breeds over most of Europe, except the far north of Scandinavia, and across Asia to Japan. In the British Isles it breeds mainly in the western half of the country, from Cornwall to north west Scotland, where it is a common sight. It used to breed in Ireland but has now disappeared from the island.

In the 19th century, buzzards suffered severely from the guns of gamekeepers, and by the end of that century they could no longer be seen in many parts of Britain. The First World War brought a change to their fortunes. There were then fewer game preserves and this allowed their numbers to recover. However, in 1954, rabbits, an important food of buzzards, were stricken with myxomatosis, and many animals that had preyed largely on rabbits went hungry. Since then the numbers of buzzards have declined, although it is now thought that the numbers are fairly steady.

Patient hunter

Buzzards hunt by pouncing on animals on the ground. They sit motionless for hours on a favourite post, tree or rocky crag, watching the ground with keen eyes. When something moves, they launch themselves into a low, descending flight on half-closed wings to seize their prey on the ground by a sudden pounce. At other times they hunt on the wing, sometimes hovering with the persistence, but not the grace, of a kestrel.

The main food of buzzards, now that rabbits are scarce, is voles, together with mice, shrews and even moles which are caught when they venture above ground. Frogs, toads, lizards, snakes and insects are also eaten, as are larger animals such as rats, stoats and hares.

Some birds are captured by buzzards, but only when the victims are caught by surprise, as buzzards are not fast fliers. Many birds have been recorded as being caught by buzzards, from pheasants, crows and little owls to yellowhammers, blackbirds and skylarks. Carrion and dead lambs are also eaten at times.

It is very unusual for an animal, other than a primate, to use tools, that is, use objects as an extension of the body to perform tasks that the body alone cannot perform. The Australian black-breasted buzzard, however, has the habit of driving ground-nesting birds off their nests to eat their eggs. The egg-shells of the emu are too strong for it to crack with its beak. Instead it flies up with a stone in its claws and drops it on the emu's nest, then descends to eat the smashed eggs.

Courtship aerobatics

In the early parts of the breeding season, birds of prey often indulge in graceful aero-

G Rüppell

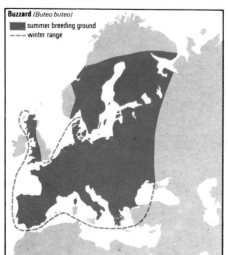

Buzzard *(Buteo buteo)*
- ▓ summer breeding ground
- --- winter range

△ *Buzzard chicks are hatched in nests built high in a tree or on a rocky ledge. At first the male brings food while the female guards the nest, but after a couple of weeks both parents hunt for food for the chicks.*

▷ *The buzzard holds down the dead rabbit with its strong feet, and tears out pieces of skin and fur with its powerful beak. The prey is then dismembered and swallowed. (Approximately ½ of lifesize.)*

batics, soaring, tumbling and looping the loop, to advertise their presence to other members of the species, or playing together to strengthen the bond between the pair. A frequent sight in the breeding season is the pair gliding in circles around each other, with the wings held up at an angle to form shallow Vs and the tails spread out. The male glides a little above the female and both face one another. This display flight shows that there is a nest nearby. At other times, the display takes the form of a repeated dive. The buzzard glides steeply down with half-closed wings then soars up again, almost vertically, to repeat the glide.

The nest is a large, bowl-shaped structure

food than the chicks can eat. The chicks leave the nest when 6 or 7 weeks old, but continue to be fed by the parents while they learn to hunt for themselves.

Tamed buzzard

In one of the books written by the Comte de Buffon, the celebrated 18th-century French ornithologist, there is an account of a buzzard kept by a curé, Monsieur Fontaine. This buzzard was remarkably tame. It wore a bell on one leg, sat on the table while the curé dined, and followed him while he was out riding. It would even bathe with the curé's ducks, but for all its tameness

The fox was killed and the buzzard had a wing broken, but it escaped and made its way back to the curé, arriving a week later in a pitiful condition.

When it had recovered from this adventure, the buzzard returned to its old habits of terrorising the neighbourhood. Although friendly with the curé's poultry, it attacked his neighbours', with the result that, at different times, it received 15 musket shots, but without serious injury. Perhaps more unpopular was its habit of stealing headgear. This was done without regard to the social position of the wearer. To quote the curé, the buzzard had a 'singular antipathy: he would not suffer a red cap on the head of

André Fatras

The buzzard belongs to the day-hunting birds of prey, characterized by the sharply hooked beak with a fleshy, often brightly coloured, skin or cere across its top.

of sticks, heather, bracken, moss, seaweed or other material, depending on locality, built in a tree, on a rocky ledge, or even on the ground on bush-covered hillsides. The nest is often decorated with fresh sprigs of foliage or ferns which are regularly replaced.

Normally, 2 eggs are laid, but up to 6 have been recorded. Very old birds may lay one only. They are incubated for 33–35 days. At first only the male parent brings food, while the female stays by the nest guarding the chicks. The male leaves the food by the edge of the nest, where it is picked up by the female and fed to the young. When the chicks are a week or so old, both parents go out foraging and sometimes bring back more

the buzzard was no coward. As an experiment, Monsieur Fontaine shut his four cats into a garden with the buzzard. He then threw the cats a piece of meat. The nimblest cat seized it, but the buzzard immediately landed on her back, hanging on with its talons and pecking the cat's ears. The cat, in her efforts to be rid of her tormentor, dropped the meat. The next cat picked it up and was, in turn, assaulted by the buzzard. Eventually the buzzard was able to snatch the meat and fly off with it.

On another occasion the buzzard was seen to attack a fox, but the keeper who witnessed this did not await the outcome. Instead he discharged his musket at them.

any of the peasants'. These were neatly whipped off and carried away, as were the wigs of the gentry, leaving them bareheaded. The plunder was then carried to the tallest tree in a neighbouring park and displayed for all to see.

class	**Aves**
order	**Falconiformes**
family	**Accipitridae**
genus & species	***Buteo buteo*** *common European buzzard* **B. rufofuscus** *auger buzzard* **B. lagopus** *rough-legged buzzard others*